We Lived a Life and Then Some

The Life, Death, and Life of a Mining Town

We'll sing a little song of Cobalt,
if you don't live there it's your fault.
Oh you, Cobalt, where the big gin rickies flow.
Where all the silver comes from
and you live a life and then some.
Oh you, Cobalt, you're the best old town I know.

"The Cobalt Song"
  – L.F. Steenman, R. L. MacAdam, 1910

We Lived a Life

Charlie Angus
and Brit Griffin

and Then Some

The Life, Death, and Life
of a Mining Town

Artwork by Sally Lawrence

and Rob Moir

Between the Lines
Toronto, Canada

Published by
Between The Lines
720 Bathurst Street, #404
Toronto, Ontario M5S 2R4
Canada

Cover illustration by Sally Lawrence and Rob Moir
Cover and interior design by Gordon Robertson

Original photographs used in artwork courtesy of the
Cobalt Mining Museum and the Bunker Museum

Printed in Canada by union labour

A contribution from the United Steelworkers of America, Miners' History
Project, toward the publication of this book is gratefully acknowledged.

Between The Lines gratefully acknowledges financial assistance from the Canada
Council, the Ontario Arts Council, and the Canadian Heritage Ministry.

Canadian Cataloguing-in-Publication Data

Angus, Charlie, 1962-
    We lived a life and then some : the life, death, and life of a mining town

Includes bibliographical references.
ISBN 1-896357-06-7

1. Cobalt (Ont.) - History.   2. Cobalt (Ont.) - Economic conditions.
3. Silver mines and mining - Ontario - Cobalt - History. I. Griffin, Brit, 1959-   .

FC3099.C6A53 1996   971.3'144   C96-931999-1
F1059.5.C6A53 1996

 20

*This book is dedicated to the people of Cobalt
who keep alive the memories of the long dead
and the otherwise forgotten.*

Contents

Acknowledgements

W E WOULD LIKE to thank everyone who took the time to sit down with us and share their stories. Our only regret is that we couldn't publish all the wonderful stories we were told—unfortunately space didn't allow it.

Rob Moir and Sally Lawrence put a great deal of energy into getting the project off the ground. Their artistic skills helped tell another part of the story.

We were greatly aided in our task by the interviews conducted in 1972 by Carmen Stubinski, Lucy Damiani, and Johanna Stubinski. They preserved many important oral memories that would have otherwise been lost.

Anne Fraboni, curator of the Cobalt Mining Museum, has done a stellar job of preserving other pieces of this rich history. Thanks for the help of Jim Jones and the Bunker. Thanks to James Urban for sharing his research materials.

Thanks to Louisa Blair for editing an unruly mass of pages. Thanks to Bob Chodos and Jamie Swift for advice.

Doug McLeod, Helene Culhane, and John Gore patiently read through the text and pointed out numerous errors.

Thanks to Vivian Hylands for the final polish and shine.

If any errors remain, the fault is ours.

Thanks to Marta Leopold, friend and supporter, and to Paul Sauvé for all the fish.

Computer assistance on the artwork came from the hard work and skill of Jamie Grant.

Thanks to Andy King and the United Steelworkers of America, District 6.

Special thanks above all to Mariah, Siobhan, Pierre, and the Griffins. Thanks to Jenny Angus for imparting a love of history.

This book has been made possible by the support of the Canada Council Explorations Grant program.

Foreword

Y OU are about to read one of the richest, most thorough, and most moving accounts of Canadian working life you will ever encounter. Authors Charlie Angus and Brit Griffin, and artists Sally Lawrence and Rob Moir, have produced a minor masterpiece in *We Lived a Life and Then Some*.

The story of Cobalt, Ontario, is a story full of fascinating characters: pioneers, prospectors, get-rich-quick artists, immigrants, brawlers, hockey players, union leaders, and families. It is most particularly a story of generations of miners and the women and children who shared their lives—lives which were lived always on the edge of disaster, always full of hope, and always with lots of laughter along the way.

Charlie Angus and Brit Griffin keep the personal and human dimension in the foreground throughout this admirable book. At the same time, they pass on a wealth of information about historical changes, economic ups-and-downs, changing work practices, labour struggles, horrifying tragedies, modest triumphs, and the patterns of daily life. The authors present Cobalt both as the unique community it is, and as a mirror through which decades of Canadian social and industrial history are reflected. And it is briskly, engagingly written, with lots of quotations and testimony from the people who made the history.

The United Steelworkers of America is proud to be able to help bring this work to public attention. In this current era of economic crisis and dislocation, more and more working people will turn to sources like this book to reflect on what came before, and on what the present struggles share with the past.

But reading *We Lived a Life and Then Some* is much more than just an important history lesson. It is also just plain good fun. So turn the page and get started. I am certain you will share my enthusiasm.

Lawrence McBrearty
National Director for Canada
United Steelworkers of America

We Lived a Life and Then Some

The Life, Death, and Life of a Mining Town

Introduction

A ROUND THE EDGES of the pool table, along the bar at the Fraser Hotel, you still hear the rumour of the motherlode. It is a matter of local faith. Someone will find the hidden motherlode. The price of silver will go up. The miners will return and the flip-chart specialists be sent packing. It is inevitable. As inevitable as the endless rock and the long winters.

Cobalt, Ontario, population 1,500 and falling, is a community that has lived and almost died by these rumours for decades. But fewer and fewer people are willing to invest in the depleted, narrow ore bodies of Cobalt. The international mining world seems to have outgrown the aged operations in the town that boasts of being the "Silver Capital of the World." For the first time in its history, a new generation of Cobalt boys aren't coming of age underground. Miners with years of experience have been forced to move or submit to MS-DOS classes in government retraining programs. Men who have spent their lives running jack-leg drills underground are now expected to begin hobbling along the information highway.

But local people still believe the old creeds. Somehow this camp will manage to produce one more mine, and this mine will be the big one. In the old days they whispered about the impending discovery of another great silver deposit. Then it was cobalt. Recently it was rumours of copper, then diamonds, and now the air is rife with stories of base metals.

It does little to argue about the improbability of such faith, or to point to the need for sustainable alternatives. Sure, people would welcome a widget factory with open arms. But they know that factories don't move to northern mining communities. They know that communities can't feed themselves on tourist dollars. And so they retain hope in the long shot because the long shots have paid off in the past.

The belief in the long shot is a fundamental tenet of hardrock mining. Farming towns don't gamble against all odds. General Motors doesn't risk its investments on the roll of the dice. But miners do. Across the country there are communities that have built their dreams on the whims of Lady Luck. They seem to possess a unique blend of machismo, optimism, and sheer stubbornness. Cobalt is one of these communities.

We discovered Cobalt while driving through northern Ontario, looking for a new home for ourselves and our two young daughters. It sits at the south end of three small communities in northeastern Ontario (known as the Tri-Towns). Compared to its scenic neighbours—Haileybury and New Liskeard—Cobalt stands out as a raw, unhealed beauty. We were drawn to its hodgepodge houses, the meandering streets, the wildflowers, and blasted rock heaps. It was as tragic as it was compelling. We had no idea that this barren town had once been the source of a silver boom that dwarfed the riches of the Klondike, a town that had yielded over $260 million in silver in its early years.

In the spring of 1990, with no job prospects or friends in the area, we packed up our children and made the move. At the time, a drop in the price of silver had put an end to the local scavenging operations underground. The iron ore mine in nearby Temagami was being closed because the steel mills in Hamilton could buy cheaper ore elsewhere. For the first time in Cobalt's history, there were no men working underground. The hills were silent. It was the silence of a fishing village bereft of codfish or a prairie town with empty grain silos. In the silence, a hard question arose: if the blasting stops and the drilling ends, what will become of Cobalt?

By all logic, the town should have died long ago. But the people remain. They remain because they believe that the mines will reopen. They remain because they have deep roots in the community. They remain, some say, because they are too stubborn to leave.

We have joined the ranks of these believers. Like many before us, we came to Cobalt on the roll of the dice. We moved with nothing more concrete than a hunch that this town was an exotic and inspiring place, a place that was meant to be ours. That was six years ago. In the intervening years we have become, as it were, addicted to Cobalt, to the rugged beauty, to the gossip around the tables at the local coffee shop, to the genuine hospitality and tolerance of this little community. Cobalt is now home.

Many studies have been done on the silver boom that took place in Cobalt from 1903-20. The emphasis has always been on the incredible wealth generated by this boom and its catalytic role in the development of Canada's powerful mining industry. But history has overlooked the story of the people and their often bitter legacy after the boom. This was where the idea of a book was born: to use the rich oral tradition of the area to reveal a culture that has lived and almost died many times.

This is in no way the final word on the people of Cobalt. We have tried to present history through the perspectives of those who have made this place their home. We believe that working-class culture can only be really understood by giving credence to local oral tradition. Only through the stories and local lore can one address the intangible dimensions of what makes a community endure.

A word of warning. Not all the stories have been recorded in this publication. Since this history is essentially a living history, we made hard decisions about which stories might be subjected to the cold and impersonal light of the page. For gaps in the oral record we suggest you consult your own community. Learn the stories over a coffee or a beer. Banish the TV and restore the spirituality of place.

1

Making a Place
in History

A S THESE MEN *from all parts of the world told the stories of the rich strikes in their own countries, I could not but ask, "With so many mines of wealth in your own and your adopted countries, why have you come to Cobalt?"*

"Ah, man, do you not know? Do you not know of the 'Miner's fever' that drives us from land-to-land—that makes us endure the cold of the north, the blizzards of the west or the hot suns of the desert? Once a prospector always a prospector. The rich strikes of the north cannot hold us when we hear of the finds in some far away land, be that land in the burning deserts of the south, or in the mountains beyond the seas. The call of the mine is siren music that bids us away, and we strike our tents and are gone, never to return."

– Anson Gard
Silverland and Its Stories

CHAPTER ONE

A Hammer and a Fox

How was silver first discovered in Cobalt?

"A fox was running in the bush and a guy threw his pick at it and it went in the road and there was all this silver," says a boy named Ben.

"No," interrupts a girl, "it didn't happen like that. The fox was by the rock when he shot the pick and he hit the rock and that's how he found silver."

What happened then?

"The guy found more silver and he built houses and signposts and people moved to Cobalt."

What happened to all the people here?

"When the money ran out, they moved away."

Now if you were going to tell somebody about Cobalt, what would you say about it?

"It's a very small town that was once very famous."

– A history of Cobalt according to the grade three students of Saint Patrick's School, Cobalt, Ontario

THERE IS A STORY told about the discovery of silver in northern Ontario and this is how it goes. When the Temiskaming and Northern Ontario Railway (T&NO) was completing the line from North Bay to the fledgling farm communities of Haileybury and New Liskeard, it had to pass through a rugged section of the shield around an area known as Long Lake. Fred LaRose was a blacksmith hired to work this section. One day in late August 1903, he was working at his forge when he was startled by a fox. He threw a hammer at the creature. The hammer missed and bounced off an outcropping of rock. When LaRose went to retrieve the hammer, he realized that the rock was a vein of pure silver.

In all probability, LaRose didn't throw a hammer and there wasn't a fox. Even though he did discover a massive vein of silver he didn't know that it was silver that he found—he thought it was copper. He also wasn't the first to make this discovery; two other railway workers, James McKinley and Ernest Darragh, had discovered silver just south of the spot almost a month before.

Such are the facts, but the story of the hammer and the fox found a place in popular history. It was repeated all over the world by men enthralled by the casual simplicity of it all. This was the era of the great gold rushes. While LaRose was labouring over the forge, the great drama of the Klondike was winding down. The Klondike was the pinnacle of a strong counter-cultural yearning that had been unleashed in the California gold rush of 1849. The California rush created a myth that incited thousands of men to leave the comforts of civilization and wander the far frontiers in search of mineral wealth. The sagas of the sourdoughs and the forty-niners were spread in stories, penny novels, and poems. Like a profane *Magnificat*, they celebrated the accidental and championed the nobody.

The story of the hammer and fox was an archetype of this tradition. Perhaps LaRose himself had heard the tale of Edward Bray. Bray unleashed the Transvaal gold rush after the shovel he threw at a black man bounced off a rock rich in gold. The fundamental tenet of the fox story was that mere luck had revealed the riches. LaRose was depicted as a caricature of the rough and simple bushman. His discovery was purely accidental, a work of fate. What if he hadn't thrown the hammer? What if his camp had been set up somewhere else? How many other men walked passed that rock without stopping to look?

In reality, Fred LaRose wasn't just a lucky rube who fell over a treasure. He took his prospecting seriously, having gained some very practical knowledge working in the phosphate mines in Quebec. He found something because he was looking. And yet the fox story implied that it wasn't skill that made the discovery, it was just being in the right place at the right time. You can't win unless you play. And you can't play unless you go there. Thousands of men did just that. When LaRose set the historical record straight to a Toronto *Globe* reporter five years later, it no longer mattered. People liked the story and the story became the history.

They say I knew nothing of mining; you say "no" to that. Since I worked as a water boy at the Buckingham mine I have worked at the rock. I am a good rock man. When I came up to Cobalt I go out whenever I have spare time and prospect. I was sharpening steel and shoeing the horses and mending the skips when they broke. There was not much spare time. It was all bush, all bush then, and there is now a fine house where my little shack was. One evening I found a "float," a piece as big as my hand, very heavy and with sharp points all over it. I say nothing but came back and the next night I take a pick and look for the vein. The second evening I found it.

    – Alexander Gray

      "Genesis and Revelation of Cobalt," Toronto *Globe*, 3 October 1908

Fred LaRose wasn't the first to discover silver in this region, but his tale has overshadowed the story of two other adventurers, James McKinley and Ernest Darragh. McKinley and Darragh made the first discovery on August 7, 1903. At the time they were working for the railway gathering timber. Both men were steeped in gold-rush lore and had once made a trek to the famous gold fields of California. Like LaRose, they found something because they were looking. While scouring for railway timbers at the south end of Long Lake, they stopped to examine some rocks showing leaves of bright metal.

It wasn't gold. They knew that. But the metal passed the only assay test they knew. As Darragh explained later in a letter, "I immediately took the advice of the old forty-niner and placed a piece between my teeth, and I succeeded in marking it very easily." After carefully staking their claim, they set about getting legal access to the land. They then sent a mineral sample off to be analyzed by an assay office in Ottawa. The results that came back were disappointing; the metal showed only traces of bismuth and arsenic. Indeed, added the assayer, if arsenic had been present in higher quantities the tooth test might have ended up in poisoning.

Although dejected, the two men were unwilling to give up. This was the closest they had come to a credible find and they decided to keep trying. Returning to the beach they sought out more samples, and this time took rocks that did not sparkle but were grayish white in colour. They sent their samples off to McGill University, to a Dr. Milton Hersey. The report brought back the news they had dreamed about for so long. What they had found was silver, and the specimen was running at a spectacular four thousand ounces to the ton!

They secured their claim and the McKinley-Darragh Mine eventually produced thirteen million dollars in silver. When the two men sold the mine out to American interests, they were careful to retain shares in the project. It was a classic success story, the rags to riches saga of two careful and reasoned businessmen. They did well.

LaRose never came close to their level of success, and yet his story personified the drama of Cobalt in a way that of the successful partners never did. The way the story is told, the gregarious LaRose sold the rights to his mine to a couple of wily shopkeepers, Noah and Henry Timmins, while waiting for a train in Mattawa. With the millions they made from the LaRose Mine, the Timmins brothers moved on to buy up the claims of a young barber from Haileybury, Benny Hollinger, who in 1909 discovered what was to become the biggest gold mine in North America. The Timmins brothers had a town named after them, and their Hollinger Mine became an economic giant. And LaRose? It appears that he returned to his forge.

There is an element of the tragic in all the great gold rush sagas. As much as they exalted the man who became a king overnight, they also immortalized the tragic return of these kings to obscurity. Whether it was Big Alex MacDonald, the King of Dawson City who died a pauper, or Sandy McIntyre, who sold a massive gold mine for drinking money, a Cinderella tale was told. The coach turns back into a pumpkin and the gown is left in tatters. But the prince never comes with the shoe.

Such myths represent a fundamental cultural break, the divide between the wild west and the settled east, between the squandering of easy money and the penny pinching ways of the careful. Diligence, sobriety, and hard-working Calvinism were the expressed values of North America's farm-based founders, but they didn't fuel the fires of the mineral seekers. The moral of the gold-rush sagas is that, for a time, these men lived glory like no others. They gambled on the longshot that brought them wealth and then, to complete the cycle, they threw their riches back into the bitter lottery of fate.

Cobalt is a daughter of such myths and exists today like a shipwrecked survivor in a surrounding sea of normalcy and prudence. The generations born and raised along its tottering streets and scarred hills carry within them the mark of a tragic glory. The nearby towns, born of patience and hard work, natter like stepsisters at the failed Cinderella, but Cobalt retains the defiance that marked the grand era of the gold rushes. They defy history with the rousing chorus "we lived a life and then some." Yes, your towns might be well-ordered and pretty, but we once entertained princes and danced on the stage of the world.

It is not without reason that such historical phenomena as the gold rushes have found their place in folk literature, for their essential elements of tragedy, disillusionment and plain human folly and weakness inevitably appeal to ordinary men as a representation in reality and on a grand scale of their own everyday fantasy lives.
  – George Woodcock, author — his father, Samuel, was a one-time resident of
    Cobalt

CHAPTER TWO

William Trethewey Comes to Cobalt

They trenched silver by day and dreamed of silver by night.

– Elizabeth MacEwan, first school teacher in Cobalt

WILLIAM G. TRETHEWEY, prospector, entrepreneur, and real-estate speculator, had a date with riches. He came appropriately attired—a suit and a white silk shirt complete with diamond pin. But since this date was in the hinterlands of northern Ontario, he put on a pair of rubber boots and brought along a rifle. Moments like this did not come very often in a man's life. Many are called, the Good Book says, but few are chosen. In the world of mining, being one of the chosen meant being one of the first.

Trethewey was a mining man. He had left his native England many years before to follow the mineral search up through the interior of British Columbia. He combined a good knowledge of geology with a flare for business and self-promotion. While Fred LaRose was pounding the forge for the Temiskaming Railway, William Trethewey was making money in the big real-estate boom going on in Edmonton, Alberta.

News of the silver discovery at Long Lake had begun to leak out over the winter of 1903-4. Willet G. Miller, the provincial geologist, examined the first finds in late fall of 1903 and was astounded by the evident wealth. Cut into the hills were rich veins of silver, discoloured with the pinkish bloom of cobalt. In his official report, he noted that silver lay on the ground like "stove-lids and cannon balls." How rich this area was, he couldn't begin to guess. But he knew that it was richer than anything previously discovered in the province.

Trethewey became aware of the discovery while on a business trip to Montreal. While visiting the office of Dr. Hersey, he had the chance to examine some of the rich samples taken from the site of the McKinley-Darragh discovery. Impressed with what he saw, Trethewey decided to stay in the east and wait for the spring thaw to come. He was determined to be amongst the first to claim the riches this land held.

On May 6, 1904, Trethewey boarded the train in Toronto. The platform was quiet. There was no mob of excited prospectors waiting. Only one other man was heading to the silver fields, Alex Longwell, who had been hired by a Colonel Leonard in Saint Catharines. Rumours of a great silver find would have emptied towns back in British Columbia, but in Ontario no one seemed to care. And these were not just rumours; they were the eyewitness accounts of the provincial geologist.

Ontario was poor soil for the seeds of adventurers and prospectors. The vast majority of its inhabitants was made up of the descendants of the settler families who cherished the stability of Upper Canada. They lived in quiet settlements huddled along the southern borders while the vast expanse of the province lay like a discarded cloak of uninhabited bush. The T&NO had only ventured through this area because a determined enclave of land-hungry farmers was trying to tame the belt of flatland running through the shield just north of Long Lake (Cobalt Lake). Known as the Little Clay Belt, this area was home to two struggling settlements—Haileybury and New Liskeard.

The financial world of Canada had little interest in stories of gold or silver. There had been finds before in Ontario, and some had staggered along for a short period, while others had been like quicksand for the gullible. Even though Sudbury was slowly being transformed into a mining mega-giant, most businessmen in Ontario remained skeptical. Chasing after minerals in the muskeg of northern Ontario was an activity fit only for fools. It was an alien tradition.

But William Trethewey was no fool. He and Longwell took the Grand Trunk to North Bay, caught the CPR east to Mattawa, from there boarded the new Temiskaming line and made the final journey into Haileybury on one of the Lumsden steamships. From there it was a five-mile walk down to the scattering of lumber and railway tents huddled along the shores of Long Lake.

The locals no doubt wondered what to make of Trethewey, who looked more like a snake-oil salesman than a prospecting man. Trethewey, however, hadn't come to get his hands dirty. He knew that there were more ways of getting rich from mining than digging in the ground. He wasn't planning to dig ore, he was hoping to promote a claim.

Trethewey was casually shown some of the veins and quickly realized that what Miller had said was true. Only no one seemed too excited about the riches that lay at hand except him.

No one at that time appeared to be very much impressed, even the fellows who made the discoveries not being at all excited, although the silver was looking them in the face. I visited the Little Silver vein from which half a million dollars in ore has been taken, and there was at least $200,000 sitting up there and looking at *them right on the surface of the vein. But they were sitting back and doing noth-ing. My idea was to buy something in the camp, but I discovered that no one was prepared to sell.*

Thwarted in his initial plan, Trethewey decided he would simply have to go and make his own discovery. He turned and headed back up to Haileybury to get the necessary supplies. Within two days he had discovered not just one major mine, but two. Just a short walk from camp, he discovered what would become the Trethewey Mine. Hav-ing come this far, he wasn't about to make any mistakes.

My first anxiety was to find if anyone had been there before me, but after careful examination I concluded it was a virgin discovery. I had no axe with me, and there were fellows down in the camp who would have made a wild rush up there if they had known, and I would have lost my mine. So I hid it as well as I could by throwing sticks and moss over the rock where I had chipped it and came down to camp and quietly had my tea. I then started out with my axe on my shoulder, slowly enough until I got out of sight of the camp and then I only hit the ground at the high places. I squared a post, put my name and the number of my license on it, planted it firmly over the discovery and made a witness tree; then I started along the bluff a little farther and discovered the Coniagas mine.

Trethewey got Alex Longwell to help him stake off these claims. Longwell then went off on his own and discovered the veins that would form the rich Buffalo Mine. When Professor Miller, the provincial geologist, examined these discoveries, he knew for cer-tain that this was a find of world-class importance. Stepping out of the scraggy bush onto the railway right-of-way, he planted a makeshift sign on an old board. It read: Cobalt Station T&NO.

Cobalt. The word means goblin. Tales of kobolds, knockers, and coblynau — crea-tures who worked in the mines—were common all over medieval Europe. These hideous, bent creatures would drill, hammer, and shovel alongside the miners. Rarely seen, they laboured mysteriously and endlessly underground, confined to a dank, damp world.

Miners told stories of encountering the kobolds at work underground and of hear-ing their distant tapping in the mines. The lore was so common that Georgius Agri-cola, writing in the sixteenth century, included some of these tales in his study of mining in Germany. Welsh miners believed the knockers were the ghosts of Jewish miners condemned to labour in the mines for their part in the Crucifixion. The Ger-mans thought these creatures lived in the rock as humans lived in the air, drawing this conclusion from the strange burning sensation the rock left in their hands after han-dling. They named this mineral after the goblins—kobold.

The lore of the kobolds follows a similar form wherever mining took place. They worked their shifts just like the miners, enduring the back-breaking work of picking and mucking the ore. And yet, for all their work underground, the kobolds never seemed to accomplish anything. There were no riches, there was no end in sight. It became a common expression to describe working without reward to say, "just like the kobolds who labour in the mines." These creatures were perhaps a tragic metaphor for the humans who laboured beside them. For all their work and dangerous toil, miners never shared in the wealth they dug.

Miller wasn't thinking of the kobolds when he conjured their presence along a barren stretch of railway in northern Ontario. And neither was Trethewey. While other mining operations in the area were stalled by the uncertainty of how to develop or market their claims, Trethewey got right down to business. He began by simply tearing rich slabs of silver off the face of the vein, bagging it and shipping it to Toronto. The sight of this rich silver was soon the talk of Toronto, and the indifference of Ontario was at an end. The myths of El Dorado and the tragic reality of the kobolds were about to be brought together in this place called Cobalt. The great silver rush was on.

CHAPTER THREE

Tents in the Bush

Cobalt sprang up in a night. Soon the woods and the lake which had long stood silent resounded with the shouts of prospectors and the tap-tap of the drill could be heard on every side . . . followed by blasts and more blasts, blasting that never seemed to cease. From a hundred clearings the camp fires by night shed their shimmering lights on the dark forest and through all a medley of music from mouth organs, concertinas, and fiddles. . . . A stirring scene it was and a refreshing picture that shattered the staid conventions of the older lands.

    – Elizabeth MacEwan

T HEY CAME with the dream of getting rich quick and getting out fast. The railway delivered men by the score, the hundreds, and the thousands. They piled off the station looking for grub, a bed, and a place to be outfitted. That the area was completely unsuited to a sudden influx of people needing accommodation and services didn't strike these men as important at all. They were willing to leave civic responsibility to the next trainload of seekers.

The early development of Cobalt resembled the standard fare of gold rush camps. In 1904, there was only a smattering of tents hovering around the seven small silver operations. Fifty-seven miners found employment in the camp in that first year. They came from faraway places like the Pacific Northwest, New Zealand, and South Africa. Within a year, sixteen mines were running, more than four hundred men were working, and well over a million dollars was taken out of the camp.

As silver discoveries continued, more and more men arrived. Men who had left behind the depleted gold fields of Alaska now bumped shoulders with greenhorns decked out in the latest prospecting gear offered by the T. Eaton Company.

The Cobalt rush was irresistible to many simply because it was so close. The Klondike could be reached only by a harrowing journey up through the Chilkoot Pass, while Cobalt could be reached by a comfortable train ride from Toronto. There were no arduous portages, no glaciers to conquer. One simply boarded the "Cobalt

Special" in the evening and awoke the next morning in the land of opportunity.

> *We got off the train at Cobalt Station October 4, 1908. The same day we got off the train a man was stabbed in the back and killed just before the train got in. When we got off the train and saw the dead man we wanted to get back on the train and go back to Buckingham.*
> – Alfred Parent, mill floation operator, 1972

> *I saw Cobalt March 17, 1906 and it was forty below. I boarded at a French boarding house. The lady gave us sowbelly and potatoes swimming in grease, doughy bread and sewage water from Cobalt Lake. Some got typhoid but I used a local intestinal antiseptic and changed houses to the Stitt House in Haileybury. Got good grub there and no lice and good treatment, but lost my patent leathers and saw them in a local saloon, the man who was wearing them was trying to push the saloon over. He had barrel fever from drinking squirrel whiskey.*
> – Frank R. Cowdery, Niles, Ohio, 1953

The railway, which was busy trying to bring work crews to the new sections of the line north of Cobalt, found that potential workers were only looking for a free ride to the land of silver. Louis Kurowski, in *The New Liskeard Story*, describes the problems this new camp was creating:

> *The bosses knew that many employees simply bought themselves a ticket to Cobalt and would be gone when Cobalt was reached. The transcontinental railway builders took special precautions when they were delivering a fresh group of workmen through the Temiskaming terrain. A common practice was for men to jump the train anywhere within a hundred miles of Cobalt. At times such as these, guards were posted at all doors, so they jumped out the windows when the train slowed down on the curves.*

Cobalt captured the public's desire to believe that a man armed only with a pick could still strike it rich. Locals loved to provide examples of individual luck and wealth. Murdoch McLeod, tramping through the bush near Kerr Lake, discovered a rich vein of silver as smooth as a sidewalk. It was tales like this that prompted men who had no experience with minerals and no knowledge of the bush to try their luck. An article in the Toronto *World* , dated April 1, 1906, relates the story of three lawyers who rode the train up to Cobalt to check it out, stayed a day, and promptly returned to the city to close up their practices and hasten back to the camp.

The newcomers were not always as well received as they might have hoped. In a stinging letter to the editor of the *Daily Nugget*, entitled "How to Go Prospecting for a

Day," Hans Buttner rebuked the disruptive presence of inexperienced and reckless prospectors. Mr. Buttner called attention to the havoc wreaked in the bush, pointing to woods littered with empty bottles, drunken prospectors, and noisy intrusions. He offered a satirical column of advice for the tenderfoot, including the following consolations:

> *If you chop off your foot by accident, be happy. It will save you the pain of having it frozen. If someone is shooting and the bullet hits you instead, do not blame anyone. You did not keep close enough to what he was shooting at.*
> *– The Daily Nugget, 11 December 1909*

Perhaps tired of being crowded in by poseurs and amateurs, Hans Buttner set off to prove how things were really done. With his partner, Sandy McIntyre, he moved onto the Porcupine and discovered a massive gold deposit; the McIntyre Gold Mine remained a major gold producer until the late 1980s.

This sudden growth of a camp that was predominantly male and transient created a serious cultural void between Cobalt and the rest of the province. The Ontario government, fearing what it knew of the wide-open boom towns of the far west, acted quickly to bring some order into the community. They outlawed the sale of liquor within five miles of any operating mine and created the first detachment of what was to become the Ontario Provincial Police force. This detachment consisted of a single police officer, George Caldbick, who met every man coming off the train and frisked him for weapons.

Early visitors had very divergent views on the extent of the lawlessness of the camp. Fredric Robson, writing in the Toronto World, proclaimed that "The order and discipline in the camp has been remarked by all who come in." Charlie Dean, an early resident, remembers it in a slightly darker manner. "When I first came I worked nights at the train station. Police supplied me with a knife, a gun, handcuffs and a billy club. I always carried the gun."

By Wild West standards, it may have seemed very civil, but in comparison to sleepy Ontario, it remained very much outside the fold. By 1911 the town had more than one hundred illegal drinking establishments ("blind pigs") operating in the camp. The Hunter Block building alone had nine bootlegging operations.

Bootleggers in Cobalt, as in the other mining communities that followed, were tolerated, respected, and often lionized. This disregard for the law chafed against the mores of conservative Ontario, and the government ultimately employed the infamous Pinkerton National Detective Agency to bust up the many bootlegging rings in the mining camp. In a 1911 editorial from The Daily Nugget, the editor complained that Queen's Park seemed more interested in lining the government coffers with fines than dealing with their own dark and dirty criminals down south. "But let a Northern Ontario hotel keeper sell two bottles of whiskey where he should have sold one and all the forces of Mr. Hanna (head of Provincial Police) and Queen's Park are bent to obtain a conviction"(Jan. 20, 1911).

Journalists commiserated with poor Mike Flynn, who received a stiff $200 fine for allowing liquor to be sold in his hotel. But that was nothing compared to the tragedy that befell the Chinese community of Cobalt. One journalist at *The Daily Nugget* described their plight:

> *There is great sorrow among the Chinamen of Cobalt because of police interference with their New Year's festivities which commence this week and last for some days, or as one of them put it so forcibly yesterday 'we get ginned for days'. . . . In the case of the Cobalt Chinamen they claim that some days ago they bought in a quantity of wine solely and wholly for this occasion. But the police got to the fact and last Friday visited a shack to the rear of the Commercial Hotel on Silver Street and seized the whole consignment.*

Besides the demand for drink, the early camp was also known for the kind of female comfort that could be had for a price. From the earliest days, cathouses were operating in Cobalt. Just as the camp was a mixture of greenhorns and veterans, so it was with prostitution. Some of the madams who moved into Cobalt had followed the trail of miners through Montana, Arizona, and the Yukon, like the "henna haired" madam who ran the Cherry Wine Inn in North Cobalt. Other women were recruited from circuits in Montreal and Toronto.

The existence of brothels, like that of blind pigs, became a common presence in the mining camps of the north. In the Kirkland Lake gold boom of the 1930s, a brothel located at 5 Main Street became almost as famous as the big mines of the region. The term "5 Main" became a common slang for prostitution among the thousands of men who passed through Kirkland Lake on their way to other employment. In Timmins, a story is told of one police chief who surprised everyone with his commitment to law and order when he busted his own mother for bootlegging and his sister for prostitution.

There is little concrete information of how these women lived. They are rendered in history as women with big hair and hearts of gold. But occasionally, a sliver of a more brutal reality can be found. One old man, telling us of his youth, said sadly, "Don't let anyone kid you. Those days were very hard. Some women who lost men in the mines had to do a lot of terrible things in order to feed their families."

The young men who stepped off the platform at Cobalt had little time to consider the darker side of mining life. They preferred to boast of the wide-open freedom offered by a mining culture. Over drinks at the bootleggers they sang of this brazen new life: "we'll riot and revel and drink like the devil, then sink down south on the train" (from "In the Cobalt Summertime"). For countless young men, Cobalt was a rite of passage. In the grand drama that was Cobalt, some would be winners and some would be losers. It was the luck of the draw.

CHAPTER FOUR

Dancing on the Stage of the World

And such a town. A collection of a thousand or so frame buildings from the modest shack to the pretentious iron sheeted hotel, strung along a curving railway for almost a mile, upon the slope of the hill above the lake (a mere pond) a smaller group of tents perched upon the summit — that is Cobalt.

Stores of every sort, law offices, banks, bowling alleys, pool room, the soft drink establishment with its more modest brother, "the blind pig," invite your patronage. And where does the business come from? From the prospecting boom. When that drops, as it must, Cobalt will be a less busy town, property will depreciate and traffic lessen. It remains to be seen if the existing mines will support a permanent town.

– Father John O'Gorman, excerpt from *The Eganville Leader*, 9 May 1906

Toronto? That's just the place you go to get the train to Cobalt.

– popular saying during the Cobalt boom

I N THE SPRING of 1904, Cobalt was merely a sign along the railway tracks. Within two years it was being heralded in the *New York Times* as "having all the sensations of the most modern city on the continent." Yet Cobalt was never a city. In many ways it wasn't even a town. It was more like a travelling show that set up a stage in the barren bush of northern Ontario and began throwing up its props and backdrops, inviting an audience of stay-at-home investors to share in the glory of the great silver rush. All they had to do was spend a little money.

And spend they did. In 1906 the area had twenty mines operating. Soon the camp was boasting over a hundred. Only forty ever really produced any silver and of these only sixteen paid out dividends. In the come-by-chance lottery of Cobalt, few were interested in the high odds of not making money, they were only interested in the odds of making money. The numbers backed them up. When the dividends were paid, they were impressive. Silver production hit $6 million in 1907, $12 million in 1909, and reached $16 million by 1912.

The first writers and journalists who arrived in the camp had continually invoked the imagery of the Klondike. But very early on it became clear that a more complex boom was taking place. Exploiting the silver deposits that lay beneath the surface required investment, development, and capital. The lone prospector with his sluice box and gold pan had no place in a land that required the blasting of hard rock and the sinking of shafts. This was a boom that would be dominated by penny stocks and promoters.

Money from outside was needed to get these silver operations off the ground. Promoters took out pages of ads in the major newspapers touting the riches of Cobalt and the opportunities awaiting with a new issue of stocks. The Toronto *Globe* printed a special sixteen-page supplement on the mines of Cobalt. The *New York Times* and New York *World* filed glowing stories on the companies that floated shares for pennies and paid back dividends in dollars.

The Temiskaming and Hudson Bay Mining Company was one such company. It owned two properties in Cobalt—the Hudson Bay Mine and the Silver Queen Mine. When the Silver Queen was sold for $800,000, Hudson Bay stock began its dizzying climb. Twenty-five thousand shares rose to $10, then to $20, and continued on until they peaked at $300 a share. It paid a return of 9,000 percent for every dollar invested!

But for every operation that proved solid, there were countless others that weren't worth the paper they were printed on. These companies, however, could still prove very lucrative to the men selling them.* Fortunes were being made by men who had never prospected or even seen a mine.

In centres like Toronto and New York, Cobalt became synonymous with quick and easy riches. Toronto was transformed by the silver boom into the new centre of buccaneer mining promotion. The starchy attitude of the Toronto business world was discarded in the dirty waters of penny stocks. Toronto remains to this day in the forefront of world mining promotion.

The foolish scramble for an interest in this mysterious district was the opportunity for certain promoters, who saw the route the sheep preferred to take, and set their traps accordingly. Cobalt has had as many 'wild-cats' exploited to the square acre as any mining district that has ever been raised as an idol to the

---

*Among the many failed promises were: the JackPot Silver Cobalt Mining Company, the Knickerbocker Cobalt, the Last Chance Mining Company, the None Such Cobalt Silver Mining Company, the Old Chap, the Rothschild Cobalt, and the Sterling Silver Cobalt Mining Company.

public. Thousands of dollars have passed from the unwise to the coffers of smiling brokers whose only claim to either the title of broker or any knowledge of mining sprang up with the Cobalt fever.
 – Frederic Robson, "Cobalt: A Mistaken Idol", *Canadian Magazine*, 1908

Toronto may have been the centre of penny stock speculation, but it was the presence of American capital that set the fire in Cobalt. From the beginning, Cobalt was a very American experience.[*] The development of the Nipissing property, known locally as the "Big Nip," illustrates the prominent role of American money. The wealth of the 846 acres that made up the Big Nip was evident back in the fall of 1903 when a bush worker, Tom Herbert, uncovered a vein of "grayish-white" rock. Herbert needed cash and had no interest in trying to develop what he found. He sold it to the only man he knew who had any money in the area, Arthur Ferland, the owner of the Matabanic Hotel in nearby Haileybury.

Ferland formed a local syndicate and bought the claim for $5,000. The Ferland group then sold the rights to an American promoter, Ellis P. Earle, for $250,000. The first excavations conducted by Earle came from an area not bigger than a house, and it yielded $350,000 in silver. Earle recognized that to get the full value of the property he would need to raise capital for a shaft-sinking operation. In May of 1906, the Nipissing Mining Company of New York started selling stock at $5 a share. Soon the Nipissing property had attracted the attention of the Guggenheim financial empire.

In October 1906 they sent John Hammond Hays, a mining engineer of considerable experience, to assess the prospects of the Nipissing property. He arrived in Cobalt in a private Pullman car. Investors throughout North America awaited his verdict. Hays was impressed by what he saw. All silver output at the Nipissing Mine had thus far come from only two surface excavations. It was clear that the property contained numerous veins. The company showed him their plans to sink twelve shafts in order to exploit the underground workings. Future potential seemed bright. The Nipissing owners had brought in experienced American managers and were clearly interested in raising the capital needed to develop a long-term mining operation.

Hays concluded that this mine would be a winner, and the Guggenheims took his advice. They agreed to buy four hundred thousand shares and purchased forty thousand straight out. They advised many of their peers to do likewise. The price of the

---

[*]A list of some of the names of companies formed in Cobalt illustrates the large American influence: the Arizona Cobalt Mining Company, Boston Portage Cobalt Silver Mines, the Cleveland Mine, the Cobalt American, Delaware Cobalt, Detroit and Cobalt Mining, Duluth Mining, the Michigan, Mississippi Cobalt, the Nevada, the New York Cobalt, the New York Ontario, the Pontiac Mining Company, the Philadelphia, the Rochester, the Southern Belle Cobalt Silver Mining Company, the Susquehanna, the Union Pacific, and the United States Cobalt.

stock soon jumped to almost $34 per share. The demand for Cobalt stocks became so intense that at one point the police had to be called out to control the crowds on Wall Street.

The snow was beginning to fall in Cobalt when the Guggenheim brothers threw a twist into the plot. On December 1, 1906, when they were obliged to purchase their second installment of shares, they announced they were dropping their option. The markets in New York went into turmoil. In two hours of trading on December 2, over seventy thousand shares were traded and the Guggenheims lost almost $2 million.

What had caused their cold feet? Some believed they were frightened off by rumours that the Ontario government might not respect the mine title and the Nipissing claim to it. Others speculated that the Guggenheims had knowledge that the Big Nip wasn't as wondrous as Mr. Hays had claimed. Many who had been stung investing in worthless Cobalt stock grumbled that it just proved Mark Twain's statement about a mine being a hole in the ground with a liar on top.[*]

If there were many wanting to get out of Cobalt stocks at the end of 1906, by the summer of 1907 there were just as many anxious to get in. The mines out at Kerr Lake were proving to be among the richest silver finds, not just in the camp but in the world. The Crown-Reserve Mining Company, the Lawson, the Drummond, and the Kerr Lake Mines were taking advantage of the rich high-grade that ran under the Lake. The Kerr Lake mine paid out over $10 million in dividends by the time it was played out in 1920.

Prospectors were fanning out throughout the region. Up on Casey Mountain near New Liskeard, silver was discovered. Forty kilometres down the Lorraine Valley a number of small silver mines were beginning in a camp known as Silver Centre. Out in Gowganda there was another silver find, and small amounts of gold had been discovered in Larder Lake.

By 1910 the money that had come out of Cobalt had dwarfed any other silver operation in North American history and had surpassed the money made in the Klondike rush. The output of silver in 1911 alone amounted to a phenomenal thirty million ounces. No longer was northern Ontario considered a wasteland. The infant steps of Canada's powerful mining industry were being made in the narrow shafts of Cobalt.

---

[*]But the Big Nip was far from finished. Indeed, it was on the verge of discovering its three main vein systems—the Kendall, the Meyer, and the Fourth of July. In 1908, twenty-seven miles of trenches were dug on the Nipissing property and thirty-three miles the following year. By the time the property was exhausted in 1950, it had produced almost ninety-two million ounces of silver and over five million pounds of cobalt.

CHAPTER FIVE

The Coming
of the Ladies

———————

"Bread or butter?" she asked.

"Bread!" I said, for I had tried the butter before.

"Ham or Eggs?"

"Ham," out of respect for old age.

"Macaroni or cheese?"

"Cheese," for I'd been there the previous week, when the macaroni they served made me think that Columbus had brought over more than he had needed and cached the surplus in Cobalt, to be discovered by a prospector.

"Coffee or tea?"

"Water."

"Can't serve water. That's extra."

"Glad of it," I said. "Glad you have something that's extra, the rest is bad enough."

"Aw, don't git smart. I mean you have to pay extra for water."

"Well then I'll take milk."

"Cow fell down the mine yesterday. Can't serve milk this morning."

– Anson Gard, *Silverland and Its Stories*

I thought this was the end of the world and I wanted to go home.

– Mrs. J. Holden, early settler, 1953

I T WAS A BUNKHOUSE LIFE. A few mines like the O'Brien and the Beaver Mines provided good services for their men, but many others offered little more than a barracks existence. Eat what the cook served up or be at the mercy of the local restaurants with their overpriced fare and bleak surroundings. In the transient world of male bush camps, such conditions were to be expected. It was often too difficult to bring families into the isolated mining camps of the west. And anyway, the men came to work, not to set up house. When the camp closed, there would be few regrets left behind.

Cobalt, however, was on the train line and close to the heartland of the country. The train made it feasible for workmen to bring their families to what would otherwise have been a distant frontier. Women brought with them the longing for home, for neighbourhood, and for community. What had begun as a fly-by-night adventure quickly took on the air of permanency.

One of the first women to arrive in the camp was Elizabeth MacEwan. She arrived in 1904 after a harrowing train trip through the north. Soon after her train left North Bay, it encountered a length of washed-out track. All the passengers had to detrain and walk across the "trestle over the dizzy ravine" to board another train. Being a women in a world of men had its advantages as she found out in her trek across the ravine: "as I was the only girl I had plenty of assistance—men to the right of me, men to the left of me—and I was properly borne across."

Elizabeth MacEwan arrived at Cobalt when "tents were giving way to shacks." What she found was a dismal sight. The landscape was a battlefield of mud, tree stumps, and rock dumps. Land was at a premium and fresh water hard to secure. The camp spilled out from the train station like tossed baggage. There were no streets to speak of, just a profusion of squatters' shacks and boarding houses limited to the narrow band along the railway or forced to seek space deeper in the surrounding bush.

Since most men worked twelve hours a day, six days a week, the task of creating a town fell on the shoulders of women like Elizabeth MacEwan. These Cobalt women were made of strong stuff. Young girls found work in the boarding houses, taking shifts that lasted from five in the morning to nine at night. Married women faced the challenge of setting up house in a tent or in a shack, raising small children in a town where water was sold by the bucket and houses had to be made out of materials at hand; dynamite boxes were a popular form of siding.

Agnes Clark and Nancy Groom learned to laugh at such things as blackflies, houseflies, mosquitoes and most other members of the insect world. They protected their babies with white cheesecloth canopies. They took for granted such things as slivery white pine floors and mud; lye soap and creek water; epidemics and fires; they helped each other through childbirth and ailments while their husbands drank and schemed down at the bars in Haileybury. They were blessed with unfailing courage, resourcefulness, generosity and above all, a

keen sense of humour, that helped them endure all the exigencies of pioneer life.
  – Maude Groom, *The Melted Years*

These women were coming to a land completely unsuited for settlement. There was no townsite, and no plan for services. People coming off the train had to fight for any available land regardless of whether it had adequate water or sewage requirements. Mrs. MacEwan relates a typical house raising witnessed by her husband:

One morning about 6 o'clock he was passing along what was afterwards called Argentite street and he saw a couple of men putting posts into the ground for the four corners of a house. When he came back at six in the evening, the house was built, smoke was issuing from a pipe put through the roof as a chimney, the family had moved in and were sitting around the table having supper.

The families needed land to settle on and a town that could provide them with basic services like schools and hospitals. Settlers in Cobalt were to find that not only were such services not provided, they had to be fought for. The chaos of the early squatters' camp was exacerbated by a government that left the civic development of Cobalt to chance and avarice. There was simply too much money and attention being centred around the mining interests of Cobalt to quibble with issues of community and settlers' rights.

Very early on, the companies realized that because of the erratic nature of the ore, they couldn't accurately assess where the veins of silver would be found. Rich shoots of silver could lie under any modest covering of moss and scrub. It became a stated policy to keep settlement as temporary as possible. They had reason to be careful. Nipissing company officials were called out to a squatter's shack when someone noticed that one of the stones used to hold up the shack looked remarkably similar to high-grade silver. The squatter, looking for foundation stones, had dug out a large piece of pure silver from a previously undiscovered vein. He was promptly evicted and his abode became the mouth for the rich Fourth of July shaft.

In order to remind the settlers that they were just temporary squatters, the mine owners set strict limits on what kind of housing could be built on their properties. The homes of the miners could only be temporary abodes. Settlers could be moved to make way for timber yards, silver exploration, or waste dumps. The land set aside for families was often land that couldn't be utilized for anything else. In the chaotic war zones of Cobalt's mine operations, families built makeshift shacks and drank out of dirty streams.

Given the high premium on land in the townsite, many miners and their families had to live some distance from Cobalt, some as far away as Latchford (ten miles to the south). Too far to walk, the miners had to rely on the T&NO, which charged high fares, ran overcrowded and unruly cars, and rarely had scheduling that was convenient for shift workers.*

Since many of the operations were out in the bush, families built shanties along their peripheries. These bush operations tended to be underserviced, and the women faced long walks into town for supplies. Beatrice Tressider recalls walking from Kerr Lake to Cobalt in snow up to her waist (a trip of about three miles). Mrs. Clorida Nixon also remembers the terrible cold of the winters:

> I remember when I was young going to church. We had five miles to go and it was very cold. And even when we went with a sleigh or a cutter we couldn't keep warm. I froze my foot once. Of course the clothing today is much warmer and more practical, then we just had cotton stockings. We didn't have proper boots; just thin wool mittens. I think we dress much better nowadays.

Although the foundations for the Stock Exchange and Opera Hall had been laid in 1905, it wasn't until 1906 that the most rudimentary school was set up. (Cobalt wasn't serviced with a high school until 1926). One of the main problems was that no trained teachers could be enticed from the south. Elizabeth MacEwan eventually took responsibility for teaching the children of this rapidly growing community. The school was built on land that had to be secured from squatters and only constant vigilance kept it clear until a building could be erected. The school opened in the early spring of 1906, with twelve students. By the end of the year there were over one hundred. They came from places as far away as Poland, Finland, Sweden, and Greece.

Mrs. MacEwan had other pressing concerns besides finding school books and a blackboard. Her task was made more challenging because her students were from all points of the globe and were of various ages. And then, of course, there were the perils of life in a mining camp.

> It was while at school that the great explosion of dynamite occurred. I had noticed wild-eyed women running by the school, hair streaming . . . but I didn't let the children see them. Suddenly there came the most terrible roar that knocked over

---

*Both the townspeople and the local media complained bitterly about the failure of this government-owned monopoly to service a region which had made it so rich. The T&NO made exceptional profits both from the sale of land, allowing the price of land to escalate far out of proportion and then selling as demands squeezed prices upward, and from the mining royalties it collected. It paid no tax to the town. Although the townsite could barely afford the basics for its citizens, the T&NO had earned some two million in mining royalties. This obvious disparity led to considerable discontent. Scathing editorials ultimately led to the largest public meeting held in the north at that time on the inequality between the north and the south, and for a time, locals began raising the issues of separating the region into a new province.

everything that was loose. It was impossible to describe our terror—some fainted and all began screaming. Crowds were running in all directions from the business part of town. Soon a man came to tell us that ten tons of dynamite had exploded and the concussion was apt to set off all the other magazines. We thought that everyone in the lower part of the town was killed. I quieted the children and sent the older ones to the lakeside—the little ones would not leave me and I could not go until I knew that my husband was safe. He was, and came running up the hill to us. . . . The men fought the fires all afternoon and night but blessed rain came and all was well again. I can still see the flames darting here and there all over the hill covered in tents.

Elizabeth MacEwan stayed on in Cobalt, teaching generations of Cobalt youngsters. When looking back on her early days in Cobalt she summed up her experience with the following:

The old days may have been hard, maybe in some cases cruel to the newcomers, but out of this struggle was born a friendliness and patriotism and love for each other that became known around the world as the Cobalt spirit . . . it was a wonderful spirit in those early days.

The struggle to build a town out of the chaos that was Cobalt would remain a hard and painful journey. Cobalt would grow deep roots and ultimately proved itself a community that could survive anything. Those who stepped gingerly off the train in Cobalt did their job well.

CHAPTER SIX

Fire and Plague

You may talk about your cities and all the towns you know,
With trolley-cars and pavements hard, and theatres where you go,
You can have your little auto and carriages so fine
But its hob-nail boots and a flannel shirt in Cobalt town for mine.

– "The Cobalt Song," L. Steenman and R.L. MacAdam, 1910

It was pouring down rain when our train pulled into Cobalt station. We tumbled out in the most disconsolate of spirits and tramped through pools of garbage heaps to the hotel. . . . Cobalt is a failure. Some first settler, if anyone knows who he was, had the bad sense to erect his home on possibly the worst piece of ground that holds up a town anywhere in America. As it stands today, there are no real streets. Huge chunks of rock in the middle of the road play havoc with the horse and vehicle that attempt a passage over them. Garbage is thrown into the backyards, cows and pigs feed on the refuse lying along the main street. There is no local water to drink. Nearly every drop consumed is brought from Montreal and sold at fifty cents a gallon. Fuel sells at exorbitant prices. Rents even of shacks run from fifty dollars to sixty dollars a month. There is no drainage, few sidewalks, scarcely any fire protection of any sort.

– Frederic Robson, *Canadian Magazine*, 1909

WHEN the provincial medical inspector arrived in Cobalt in 1905, he was appalled by the conditions. No sewage facilities existed, and public washroom facilities were extremely limited. In the unregulated camp, people disposed of both garbage and night-soil in whatever fashion they could. Garbage was dumped from second- and third-story windows into the alleyways, animals as large as horses and cows were left for dead in the town streets and laundry drains and lavatories drained into the streets. Many water sources were undrinkable because of contamination from mining operations. People drank out of the streams that others used to dispose of their sewage. By the summer of 1905, the townspeople of Cobalt Lake were infested with intestinal bacteria.

According to Maude Groom, in her book *The Melted Years*, there was only one toilet available for every twenty-five people. She relates the story of a gentleman who found himself in need of the public toilet on Prospect Street. The charge was five cents. He handed the attendant a dime only to be told there was no change. "That's all right," the man replied, "have a crap on me."

> *Garbage, wash water, urine, and feces were all mixed together in frozen heaps in the open, on top of rock practically bare in its greater area. The cold has been steady so far and all is frozen, but when the thaws come the accumulations will all be washed into the valleys and the lake, polluting all water sources. If nothing is done . . . then in all human probability there will be a severe outbreak of disease in and about the settlement.*
>
> – Report of the Public Health Inspector, 1905

In 1906 Cobalt was beset by the first of many epidemics. "Men died so rapidly," recalled Elizabeth MacEwan, "that each morning showed the dead laid along the roadside waiting for removal. It was hard to fight the sickness because no real sanitary conditions [existed]." Temporary hospitals known as pesthouses were set up on the outskirts of town. Medical personnel, afraid of spreading the disease any further, left the victims to fend for themselves.

Against this backdrop of a colossal health disaster, a Town Council was formed.[*] Early Town Council meetings were full of warnings of new outbreaks of fever and the dangers that lay in continued use of dirty water. But the fledgling town councillors were no match for the collusion of money and government. According to Douglas Baldwin in his essay "The Development of an Unplanned Community: Cobalt, 1903-1914," the community was basically destitute because it was unable to tax the spectacular mining revenues. Provincial policy at the time assessed companies only at their head offices. The Town Council repeatedly pointed in frustration to the many companies that avoided paying taxes altogether because the province had no system of locating the head offices.

The mine owners treated the residents with complete disregard. In 1908 the Town Council tried to get a legal injunction to stop the discharge of waste from the Coniagas mill. The discharge often flowed down Argentite Street (a main shopping district) and at times flooded out homes. A year later, a major public works project was delayed

---

[*]Because voting rights were tied to land rights, only 144 voters were eligible to vote out of a potential voting population of 4,000.

because Colonel Leonard of the Coniagas company refused to agree to the building of a public sewer near his property unless he was given the right to blow it up whenever he deemed necessary and not be liable for any damages.

Colonel Leonard typified the attitudes of absentee owners who treated not only the residents, but also the businesses and the civic infrastructure of the town, as mere squatters. In 1914, the Coniagas sank a shaft right on busy downtown Silver Street. The waste rock dumped in behind the shaft soon became a threat to nearby businesses. The Coniagas officials informed Jamieson Meat Market (which was located beside the slag dump) that responsibility for building a trestle to move the waste rock lay with the meat market. Jamieson refused, and his store was buried under the weight of rock.

The pressures of a growing population and the free-for-all nature of the many mining operations made for a very dangerous situation. In 1906, an explosion of dynamite tore up a section of town, and the makeshift shanties were easy prey to fire. Civic officials warned that a serious fire threat remained if houses weren't repaired and proper water lines installed.

On July 2, 1909, their fears were realized when a fire broke out in the New York Cafe in the neighbourhood of Frenchtown. According to the *Daily Nugget*, the fire tore through the north end of town "among the shacks of the Finns." The winds pushed the fire down the crowded back alleys and through the ramshackle boarding houses of Frenchtown. As buildings were devoured by flames, people frantically attempted to save a few possessions and escape. "Right by the side of the track, household goods were stacked by wailing Syrians and Greeks but it was to no avail." Nearly two thousand people were left homeless. Almost half the town was a charred, desolate wasteland.

Typical of the Cobalt spirit, the *Daily Nugget* proclaimed the following day that the town would rise "phoenix-like from the ashes," to rebuild bigger and better. It was a grand boast that might have brought comfort to anxious investors far away, but it rang hollow among the destitute who were now living in tents, subject to further deteriorating sanitation.

Unwilling or unable to pay for the high cost of clean water, many homeless families relied on local stream water. As the summer wore on, new signs of typhoid were reported. It wasn't long before the town was in the throes of the worst typhoid epidemic in Ontario's history. As before, the lack of public planning and poor health facilities made the situation much worse than it needed to be. A public health nurse who had come up from Toronto was so outraged that she told the *Daily Nugget* that many deaths from this latest epidemic "were nothing short of manslaughter."

Mrs. Saunders was the first nurse in Cobalt. She was helped by Jessica Dixon, the young wife of a mining engineer.[*] As the epidemic spread, the young women could

---

[*]Beverly Dixon Mallette, granddaughter of Jessica Dixon, has recently written a novel about her grandmother's experiences in early Cobalt, entitled *Jessica* and published by the Highway Book Shop.

not keep up. Over 1100 cases of typhoid were reported in the town. The primitive medical facilities were no match for the numbers. Tents had to be set up on Nickel Street, surrounded by the ever present mud.[*]

The cost of the epidemics and fires added to the burden of the town. Complaints to the government fell on deaf ears. One letter from the Town Council to government minister Frank Cochrane made the complaint: "It's not fair to the town for the government to treat us this way. The government should at least give us streets to walk on and have a little consideration for the immense municipal problems that are facing us."

No help was forthcoming. The government of James Whitney had no intention of letting the needs of residents stand in the way of potential profits from the silver operations. In 1906, controversy erupted at Queen's Park over the ceding of the mining rights to Cobalt Lake. Willet Miller had originally exempted the lake from staking because he recognized that a growing town would need access to fresh water. The debate at Queen's Park was not over whether the lake should be mined or not, but who should get to mine it and how much the government could charge. Sir Henry Pellatt's Cobalt Lake Mining Company paid a spectacular million-dollar fee for the right to drain Cobalt Lake. None of that money was used to compensate a growing community for the loss of their fresh water supply.

In 1913, desperate to increase its tax base, the town allowed the McKinley-Darragh Mine to drain what was left of Cobalt Lake, providing the mine agreed to be annexed into the town limits. Taxes garnered by this move helped stabilize the situation in town, but it also left a large mud pit stinking of dead fish in the centre of town.

Cobalt Lake has never really recovered from the mining operations carried out along its shores. The lake is only a fraction of its former size. The hills of the nearby Nipissing properties remain bare and scarred from the hydraulic hoses that blew the vegetation off the hills in the frantic search for silver. The only visible sign of Cobalt's wealth is in Toronto, where a garish castle built with profits from Sir Henry Pellat's Cobalt Lake mining operations continues to draw thousands of tourists every year. Visitors to Casa Loma come to hear how Sir Henry built the castle for his loved ones and then went broke trying to maintain it. They don't hear about the lake in northern Ontario that yielded Sir Henry his wealth and was left for dead once the wealth was taken.

---

[*]The result of these latest disasters finally compelled the principal power brokers in Cobalt to take action. The Cobalt Water Commission was formed. Clean water from nearby Sasaginaga Lake was pumped into the town of Cobalt. Strict by-laws were enacted to keep Sasaginaga Lake clean from pollution and sewage. The Water Commission has remained in effect since 1910 and it continues to ensure that Cobalters have one of the cleanest water supplies in northern Ontario.

CHAPTER SEVEN

Featuring a Cast of Thouands

We've got the only Lang Street there's blind pigs everywhere.
Old Cobalt lake's a dirty place, there's mud all over the square.
We've got the darndest railroad, it never runs on time.
But it's hob-nail boots and a flannel shirt in Cobalt town for mine.

– "The Cobalt Song," L. Steenman and R.L. MacAdam, 1910

OLDTIMERS, looking back on the first days of Cobalt, remember the excitement. The fires and the squalor recede with memory, but what remains is the sense of a young town bursting with exciting characters and new neighbourhoods. The vividness of those memories would always be punctuated by the singing of "The Cobalt Song." Written in 1910, the song bragged of the wild frontier life and quickly became the anthem of Ontario's new boom town.

By 1909 the town boasted a rag-tag downtown full of tailors, dressmakers, haberdashers, and ice-cream makers. The merchants, like the miners, came from all over the world. There were Russian Jews, Syrians, and Greeks. They came because they guessed that mining money was spending money. Soon there were over a hundred shops operating down Swamp Street and up Lang Street.

The merchants gave flavour to the developing community. The town mirrored a city with its designated neighbourhoods like Frenchtown, Pigtown, and Swamp Street. These were the enclaves of the Ukrainians, Finns, and French. Amongst the mining operations scattered out in the bush, small communities of workers and their families sprang up. Each one had its own character and identity.

The ethnic diversity in Cobalt underlined the divide between the mining towns and the dominant culture in the rest of the province. Ontario at that time was still rooted in its Protestant "Orange" heritage. It was conservative and agricultural. Immigrant families arriving in Toronto (called Little Belfast because of its militant Orange nature) found that well-paying jobs were often the exclusive reserve of Anglo-Scots.

According to Maude Groom, the first settlers in the Haileybury region shared this attitude. They were determined to prevent settlement by French-Canadian Catholics from across the lake in Quebec. The pioneer P. T. Lawlor, known as Protestant Tom, was very vocal in his desire to "keep the Catholics from pouring in." When two francophone loggers, Peter and Fred Giroux, attempted to open a logging road in the Haileybury region, they met the full force of Orange resistance. P.T. Lawlor led a mob armed with axe handles and cant-hook butts against the two loggers. Both men were beaten unconscious and Peter died of his wounds.

The sudden influx of newcomers brought out the tension between a conservative Anglo-Scots Protestant culture and a growing immigrant Catholic presence. Some mines tried to maintain a policy of not hiring Catholics, but as the demand for labour increased, the hiring practices had to become more inclusive. Soon Cobalt was drawing on the large labour pool of the recently emigrated, as well as families from Quebec, the Ottawa Valley, and the Maritimes.

Skilled trades jobs remained the domain of Anglo-Scots Protestants. To be hired as a machinist, or a shift boss in any of the big operations, usually meant proving membership in the Orange Lodge (a situation that often continued up into the 1960s at some mines in the north). Underground, the better-paid jobs of drilling often went to Swedes and Norwegians. The timbermen were often Finns. The hard jobs of mucking and tramming out the ore were usually the domain of the Italian and French miners.

But on the shanty streets of Cobalt, immigrant children played, fell in love, and intermarried. Children of British heritage grew up learning Italian songs and eating cabbage rolls and borscht. When many of these families joined the trek to Timmins, Kirkland Lake, or Val d'Or, they no longer called themselves Finns or Poles, but preferred to say they were Cobalters.

The burgeoning population also created a demand for entertainment and recreation. Despite its horrendous public health situation, Cobalt maintained a facade of gentility and culture. Tennis courts were fashioned beside the waste dumps at the Coniagas. On the Nipissing property, a private zoo was set up full of exotic animals. They lived in cages up on the hill beside the timber yards and the mine track.

And of course there were the theatres. Culture was paraded in theatres like the Bijou, the Lyric, the Grand, the Orpheum, and The Idle Hour Theatre. Haileybury Road was renamed rue de l'Opera. The famous actor from England, Sir Herbert Beerbohm Tree, made an appearance, as did Europe's Cherniavsky Trio.

As the town began to grow exponentially, so too did the need to provide adequate services. The Bank of Commerce set up its first branch in a tent. When they made the move to a real bank building, the managers had to resort to taking the windows out on pay day so the miners could get in and out more quickly. It is said that the restaurants were so busy that one owner operated twenty-four hours a day, only closing when he ran out of pots.

In 1910, a streetcar line was opened to connect Cobalt with nearby Haileybury and New Liskeard. It ran every fifteen minutes from early in the morning until midnight. In its first nine days of operation, the streetcar line carried thirty thousand passengers. With mining communities growing up at Kerr Lake and Giroux Lake, streetcar service was extended into the bush. Even the new town of Silver Centre, forty kilometres down the Lorraine Valley, had regular service.

The culture that developed in Cobalt was well spiced with a casual acceptance of outrageous rumour. People believed in the fantastic and perhaps this is what made otherwise ordinary events develop into almost mythic proportions. This was personi-fied in the presence of a stray mutt that was named Cobalt the Dog. This little bulldog could have lived the typical life of a stray, sleeping in doorways and getting food on the sly. Yet Cobalters looked upon the mutt as a talisman of great fortune. No hotel or restaurant would refuse the dog a meal. Indeed, his presence in a hotel keeper's lobby was a sign of great prestige. When Cobalt the Dog followed prospectors into the bush, people took it as a sign of good luck. He often rode the streetcar up to Haileybury and would occasionally board the ferry, *The Meteor*, to take the trip over to Quebec. The dog always made it back, caught the return streetcar and came home to Cobalt.

The dog was a regular on the train to Toronto. No one is quite sure what Cobalt the Dog did on his short jaunts to the big city, but he would always reappear in the hustle and bustle of Union Station to catch his train home. When Cobalt the Dog was fatally injured in a fight with a less illustrious mutt, news of his medical condition displaced reports from Flanders as the front-page story in the local press. Seventy-five years later, Cobalt the Dog stories persist, and the local mining museum proudly displays his ugly mug on their t-shirts.

> We bet our dough on hockey and swore 'til the air was blue,
> the Cobalt stocks have emptied our socks with dividends cut in two.
> They won't get any of our money in the darned old Porcupine
> for it's hob-nail boots and a flannel shirt in Cobalt town for mine.
> – "The Cobalt Song," L. Steenman and R.L. MacAdam, 1910

Mining culture by its very nature is a gambling culture. Men bet serious money on which way a fly would land on the table, or who would be the next to be blown up un-derground. Sporting events were the ultimate sources of gambling hysterics. The mines hired top-quality athletes from all over to play on their teams. Gerald McAn-drew's father was hired by the Nipissing Mine because of his skill as a ballplayer. "In those days the mines brought in players from the United States and all over. On the ball team my dad was the only Canadian player, the rest were all Americans. The day of the game they would go to work for an hour and then were sent back home to rest up for the game. He never really had to work hard at the mine. I'd say he had it made."

In Cobalt, hockey was a religion. As the oldtimers tell it, there was a time when the entire payrolls of some of the mines would be locked in the safe at the Matabanic Hotel in pregame betting. Besides the many different teams sponsored by the local mines, the town had the famous Cobalt Silver Kings, a team that competed in the National Hockey Association against teams like the Ottawa Senators and the Montreal Wanderers. Nearby Haileybury also sponsored a hockey team. There was an intense rivalry between Cobalt and its prettier neighbour. The miners lived in Cobalt and the managers lived in Haileybury. The coveted prize for teams in this era wasn't the Stanley Cup, it was the silver O'Brien trophy made from rich Cobalt ore.

In the 1909 finals, the Silver Kings paid Art Ross (namesake of the famous trophy) $1,000 a game to upset Haileybury. Dr. Eddie Phillips, the referee for the affair, kept his pregame remarks short and sweet: "Boys," he said, "the sight of blood is nothing new to me." After the carnage was over, Cobalt took home the O'Brien trophy.

In 1910 Cobalt faced its archrivals in Haileybury once again. Mining magnate Noah Timmins is believed to have wagered over $40,000 (a staggering amount for those days) on the game. Two other Haileyburians apparently mortgaged everything they owned. These were serious sporting men. And they weren't alone. Miners rushed to place their penny-ante bets. More than one Irish housewife would be lowering the boom if the Silver Kings went down to defeat.

At midgame, Cobalt led by five goals. Timmins went into the Haileybury dressing room and promised one thousand dollars, a year's wages down in the shafts, to any man who could score the winning goal. Leslie McFarlane, who later went on to pen the Hardy Boys mysteries, remembered the 1910 final as "the roughest period of hockey ever played anywhere." Haileybury came back with five unanswered goals sending the game into overtime. When Haileybury player Horace Gaul got the puck past the Cobalt goalie, pandemonium broke out. ". . . the Haileybury fans emptied their pockets and hurled money onto the ice. Paddy Moran rushed into the dressing room and returned with a large washtub, scooped up all the money he could find, tossed it into tub, then turned the tub upside down and sat on it."

On the chipped ice of Cobalt's rinks, children's games were turned into epics, muckers and hoistmen transformed into heroes. But the magic couldn't last. Even as the great Haileybury-Cobalt epics were being played out, people were beginning to turn their attention to the rumours of a great gold find at Porcupine Lake. The discovery of the Dome Mine in 1909 was the beginning of the biggest gold find in North American history—the Porcupine gold camp. The story of Fred LaRose suddenly paled alongside the discoveries by men like Benny Hollinger and Sandy McIntyre.

Gold fever began to drain the money out of Cobalt. The gold-hungry eyes of investors turned to the previously ignored bushlands farther north. Within two years the first finds of rich gold veins were made along the shores of Kirkland Lake. The *World Magazine* of New York described the ascendancy of this new gold region.

> *The song of gold has taken the place of silver in Northern Ontario, and the sound has gone the world around. Now the Song of Gold is playing its Loreli notes in a new quarter of the world—North Ontario—and as over the slopes of Sierras, on the fastness of Africa, the bleakness of Alaska and the deserts of Nevada.*

Ambrose O'Brien, son of the Cobalt silver czar, M. J. O'Brien, saw the writing on the wall. He began the breakup of the Eastern League with the newly formed National Hockey Association. The Silver Kings joined this league and played against O'Brien's newly formed French-Canadian franchise, the Montreal Canadiens. But after two seasons, the silver capital was finding it hard to keep up with the bigger centres like Toronto and dropped out.

The new gold towns would be bigger, better organized, and provide infinitely more riches than had ever come out of Cobalt. But they would never be nearly as magical. Many of the people drawn to the new camps would hear the old hands tell of the grand old days of Cobalt. When maudlin voices were warmed up with liquor and memories, "The Cobalt Song" would be sung, and the tales of the legendary Silver Kings told. Such lore would test the credulity of newcomers who could not believe that a town grown so quiet and poor had played against teams like the Montreal Canadiens.

CHAPTER EIGHT

Big Jim McGuire

*I had the pleasure of knowing Big Jim McGuire. He was a powerful man.
I went a few years ago to try and find his grave, but unfortunately the
graveyard is getting bigger all the time.*

– Mike Farrell, retired union activist, 1993

I N THE SPRING of 1909, the *Daily Nugget* printed a list of men who had
made fortunes in the mining camp. Thirty-five millionaires spawned
from an estimated working population of three thousand miners. The
millionaires, of course, would not reside in the mining camp. Most preferred to remain in their home towns, New York, Buffalo, Toronto, and Chicago. They could visit
the silver town via the "Millionaires Express," a T&NO train complete with elegant din-
ing and library cars.

The big money wasn't in evidence on Cobalt's muddy streets. While there was
never a shortage of the rich and would-be rich visiting the ramshackle silver town, the
closest the well-to-do would come to living in the area was in scenic Haileybury,
where a row of beautiful homes graced the picturesque shore of Lake Temiskaming. It
was a far cry from nearby Cobalt, where the men had to drink in illegal bootleg joints
and risk their lives in the daily struggle of hauling wealth from underground.

As injuries mounted and the cost of living continued to be one of the highest in
Ontario, the miners began to demand a fairer share. Many of the miners and mine
managers were veterans of the labour wars in Colorado and Idaho. Some of the most
bitter and violent labour battles in American history had taken place in the mining
camps of the Pacific Northwest. Of all the American unions, the Western Federation
of Miners were seen as the most radical. The mine bosses fought the union with the
Ku Klux Klan, the Pinkertons, and vigilante gangs. The union fought back with their
"powder men." More than one mine manager was blown sky high by a tripwire and dynamite. More than one mining operation was put out of commission permanently by
a cage full of blasting powder.

In March of 1906, Paddy Fleming, formerly of the Virtue Mine in Oregon, called a general meeting to discuss grievances. One of the main issues was the fact that the owners of the many different mines had formed an association of their own. The Temiskaming Mine Managers' Association was more than a gathering of mining interests — it worked to keep wages constant, and the mine managers had set up a hiring system to keep known undesirables like western activists out of the local workforce.

The miners decided to form the Cobalt Miners' Union (Local 146 of the Western Federation of Miners). The spectre of the WF of M sent a chill through investors and mine owners. Local 146 represented a new face of unionism in eastern Canada. With a mandate to fight for the rights of all workers, and not just the skilled, this fledgling miners' organization stood apart from the closed craft unions that existed elsewhere in the province.

Labour activist and historian Jim Tester believes the Cobalt Miners' Union played a very important role in transforming trade unionism in the province. "Although it hasn't really been recognized, I think the record will show that the Cobalt Miners' Union was the most militant and best-informed local of all the WF of M locals in North America. Their political enlightenment was on a very high level. They supported more strikes with voluntary dues payments, supporting Mexican-American workers for example, than most of the locals in the United States."

James McGuire (known locally as Big Jim) was a main organizer of the Local. His first challenge was to build links among the growing and diverse immigrant population. Some historians believe that the mine owners of northern Ontario, following in the footsteps of their ilk in the United States and South Africa, deliberately hired as many different ethnic groups as possible to create a Tower of Babel that would defy unionizing drives.

> *Mine foremen often play national prejudices to get men to do more work in the mines, such as putting a gang of Finlanders in one drift and a gang of Swedes in another drift, and then the foremen tells the Swedes how well the Finlanders are doing and the Finlanders how well the Swedes are doing.*
> – W. H. P. Jarvis, *Trails and Tales in Cobalt*

Bob Carlin arrived in Cobalt as a teenager fresh from a farm in the Ottawa Valley. He remembers that the hiring of miners reflected a very deliberate policy of maintaining ethnic imbalance. "If you hired two men and the two men were Irish, you would try to get one that was Irish Catholic and one that was Irish Protestant. You couldn't bring the two together and so it was a guarantee certificate that you would never have a union." This ethnic divide was promoted throughout the labour force between Protestant Orange shift bosses and Catholic French or Irish workers, between Serbs and Croats, between Red Finns and White Finns.

Cobalt became a testing ground to see whether men of so many differing nationalities could stand together as one. The test wasn't long in coming. The Temiskaming Mine Managers' Association refused to meet with the union and ignored a call for an improvement in hours and wages. The men worked six ten-hour shifts a week for $3.25 a day. What they wanted was six nine-hour shifts at $3.50 a day.

On July 2, 1907, three-quarters of the men from forty mines and mills walked out. Within two days, the five companies owned by Canadians settled and the workers returned.* The American operations seemed intent on carrying on the war they had left behind in the far west. The Pinkertons were brought in, but the lawless vigilante justice that was allowed in the United States wasn't given much chance to flower in conservative Ontario. The Cobalt Miners' Union was certainly a far cry from the "Direct Action" philosophy of its affiliated union, the Wobblies (Industrial Workers of the World), and yet local media were more than willing to paint Local 146 as a dangerous menace to democracy.

Initially the Temiskaming Mine Managers' Association tried hiring replacements from the large pool of semi-employed coal miners in Nova Scotia. When these men were brought in, however, they refused to cross the picket lines. The union assisted them in returning home. Other scabs were brought in from down south. Miners fought back in pitched battles along the rail lines until finally the mine owners smuggled the scabs in at Martineau Bay using the steamship *The Meteor*.

John. P. Murphy writes that once these strikebreakers were safely ensconced in the bunkhouses, the Temiskaming Mine Managers' Association announced that these replacement workers would be paid $3.50 a day and have to work only nine hours, the same rate demanded by the strikers. What was at stake was not the issue of wages, but the very existence of the union. As Douglas Fetherling points out in *The Gold Crusades: A Social History of Gold Rushes*, the mine owners in Cobalt had an "almost pathological" fear of the union and were adamant that they would not recognize the WFM.

The strike dragged on, and the workers began to feel the pinch. Bob Carlin relates that when funds were dwindling, the miners looked to Big Jim to solve their problems.

During the first strike when they started to get a little hungry, the miners began to say, "We've had nothing to eat for 4 or 5 days now and the kids are getting hungry. If I had a nice blue suit like you McGuire, I'd go up to New Liskeard and see the chicken farmers. Surely you could get them to donate three or four dozen eggs." So McGuire put on his blue suit, the only one he had and he went up to the

---

*The owners of the McKinley-Darragh Mine, for instance, agreed to union terms because they were in the process of selling out to the Rochester-based Kodak Company. They feared a strike would scuttle the sale.

*Catholic Church there, because he was a devoted Catholic. He stood outside the
church and started speaking on a little soap-box. He called to the people as they
were coming out of church, telling them about the great struggle for democracy.
He said a threat to democracy anywhere was a threat to democracy everywhere.
He was telling them that the most sacred thing they could do was to feed the poor.
But these weren't union people, they were farmers. And the eggs started to come. I
remember him telling me, "I got enough eggs on my nice blue suit to feed all the
strikers and their families."*

The mine managers had McGuire arrested and sentenced to six months in jail on the
pretext of violating the *Industrial Disputes Act*. The strikers were hungry and had run
out of reserves. But the workers weren't the only ones feeling the repercussions of the
strike. Accident rates soared in the scab-operated mines and the output of silver
dropped dramatically. The strike fizzled and the men gradually returned to work.

The absence of a clear resolution between the union and management only set the
stage for further confrontation. The owners blacklisted good union men to try to rid
their payrolls of activists. And according to Carlin, in the dark of the mine, some miners settled scores with those who had chosen to scab.

In 1911 the Farmers Bank (which owned the Keeley Mine) collapsed and the miners in Silver Centre lost all their savings and their wages. The syndicate that took control of the mine added insult to injury by a demand for a cut in pay. The miners went
on strike and the newspapers were once again full of talk of the Red threat.

Local 146 was never able to win a clear showdown with the companies, but many
important concessions were won by their determination. In 1912, Chief Justice Meredith came to Cobalt as part of a Royal Commission on the need to establish a government compensation program for injured workers. Local mine managers ridiculed the
idea. When it came time for McGuire to make a presentation, he did it in no uncer-
tain terms. Jim Tester believes that McGuire played a significant role in the passing of
the Compensation Act.

Big Jim McGuire was probably most responsible for the Compensation Act
*being passed in the province of Ontario. It came out of Cobalt, essentially. But
this knowledge has been lost. No one today remembers why there was a need for
independent coroner's juries to be brought in to investigate accidents or the need
to develop a no-fault insurance policy that protected the worker. But it was
prompted because the companies took very little responsibility and very little ac-
countability for conditions in their operations. Prior to the* Workman's Compensation Act *a man had to present himself as a whole man, ready for a full day of
work. If he was injured and unable to work, he was let go. The struggle of the
Cobalt Miners' Union had very deep social implications. It affected the whole of*

society. And the fact that Cobalt should be the key area for the whole trade-union movement throughout Canada is a significant thing. I think not nearly enough credit has been given to the Cobalt miners.

Bob Carlin recalls that the Cobalt Local was the centre of union activism in the north and helped establish other locals in Silver Centre, Gowganda, Porcupine, and Boston Creek. In 1913, McGuire went down to Toronto with Bill Thompson (Porcupine Local) and Charley Lothien (Silver Centre Local) to lead the fight for the eight-hour day. These victories helped open the door for workers in less militant sectors.

The idealism of the era is perhaps best captured in a photograph taken during a 1912 strike of the Porcupine miners. The photograph shows miners marching on a frigid day past the office of the Western Federation of Miners. They carried red signs emblazoned in a myriad of European languages as they filed past the union hall with its huge banner exhorting the "Workers of the World Unite."

But such idealism couldn't last. In August 1914, the world mobilized for war in an air of excitement and naiveté. Men rushed to join up, fearing the adventure would end before any of them got a chance to see some fighting. Captain E. F. Armstrong raised a battalion in Cobalt and surrounding districts. Men tired of the slowdown in the silver boom looked upon the war as the chance for another great adventure.

In November 1916 Armstrong and his one thousand men landed in England. With typical northern Ontario bravado, they brought with them as live mascots a bear and a moose. But the great lark in Europe soon proved to be a charnel house of flesh and ideals. Within three months, the unit was broken up and the men used to fill the ranks of decimated units along the Somme frontier. When the survivors returned to Cobalt at the war's end, the struggle in the mines was still going on. And the world had grown meaner.

CHAPTER NINE

The Whistle Blows
Nine Times

You could see strings of light in the morning. It was the miners going from
the mines to the various cook houses. The lights were carbide lamps on
their hats; they came in every direction.

All the mines had whistles that blew the start of the shift in the morn-
ing, quitting time, at twelve, again at one and then at five. On New
Year's Eve all the mines blew the old year out and the new year in. Each
whistle was different. You could identify the mine by their whistles. In
case of an accident, it was nine blasts on the whistle and people would
know then where to go.

– Leo O'Shaughnessy, mine owner and mill superintendent, 1972

J OHN SHANNON never had a chance. It was the first week of the new year
of 1909 and he was working his usual shift in the number one shaft at
the Crown Reserve Mine. The rounds (a sequenced dynamite explosion)
had been blasted in the rock face, creating a pile of broken rock. It was Shannon's job
to get in amongst this rubble with his shovel and "muck" it into the ore car. It was
backbreaking work at the best of times, but this morning it was worse. While carrying
out the simple job of shoveling rock, he had inadvertently picked a piece of unexploded gelignite. The rock exploded, and John Shannon became the first statistic of
the new year.

Shannon was joined two days later by Pete Peterson, who fell off a rope while sink-
ing shaft over at the Davis Silver Mine. Less than a month later, on February 2, Will
Stafford was attempting to get into the cage between the second and third levels of the
City of Cobalt shaft when he slipped and plunged to his death.

March saw deaths at three different mines, all from failed blasts or rounds that went
off too early: Ainslie Patriquin struck gelignite with his shovel in the Temiskaming

Mine on March 3, Robert Johnson was caught in a blast at the McKinley-Darragh on March 17, and John Bailey was blown up in the Elgin Cobalt on March 30.

On May 25 John Pirttinen slipped from the bucket in the Fourth of July shaft and fell to his death. Four days later at the Cochrane Silver Mine, two brothers, Ronald and John McDougall, were drilling into the rock face when they drilled into a hole that contained unexploded dynamite. John was seriously injured; Ronald died.

Over at the Nova Scotia Mine two weeks later, Alerio Marinelli was killed by a boulder that fell on him while he was trenching. The following week, Henry Davis, a teamster at the Badger Mine, was crushed between the timber and the cage while trying to get into the cage.

The Crown Reserve recorded its second fatality of the year on July 4 when two pipefitters fixing a pump at the second level were overcome by poisonous fumes. A round had been set off the previous night down the drift and no fresh air had been pumped in. Frank Malone and Fred Dyer were sent down the next morning at 8:30. Crews on the first level became alarmed when they didn't hear anything from the men and rushed down only to find that they had been overcome by the fumes of the blast. Dyer lived; Malone didn't.

Four days later, back at the Nova Scotia Mine, Samuel Chislett was crushed between the cage and the timber. On August 8 Frank Creen was sinking a shaft at the Temiskaming Mine when a rock fell from the bucket above him. He was killed instantly. Over at the Farah Silver Mine on September 17, Euclide Vicente fell out of the bucket to his death. He apparently was overcome by poisonous fumes from a blast. Five days later Elinder Eliason was killed by the cage in the Cobalt Central shaft.

On October 5 the nine blasts of the whistle were sounded at the Big Six Silver Mine in nearby Gowganda for D. H. McGillivray. He had lit his round of charges and was trying to get into the bucket to get away, but the blast went off prematurely and so did he. The year ended the way it began, with a blast. An explosion in the Rochester Mine on December 29 sent the mangled body of Ernest Bailey to join John Shannon and the rest of the sad graduates of the class of 1909.[*]

Yet all in all it wasn't a bad year for accidents. The year before, thirty men had been killed in the mines of Cobalt. Most of the deaths were unpredictable. Even if you took all the precautions, the spectre of death and disfigurement hung in the drifts like an ever-watchful demon. In some ways, it all came down to a matter of luck. Was this the

---

[*]The Ontario Department of Mines listed the 1909 fatal accidents in its 1910 report. Even though it names the seventeen men listed above, there were seven more Cobalt fatalities not listed. They are: J. Holland, killed at the Crown Reserve by falling timber; Herbert Cooper, asphyxiated in the O'Brien Mine; Joseph Scott, fell down the shaft at the O'Brien; George Puckett, drilled into hole containing dynamite at the McKinley-Darragh; Costen Ruciarz, blown up after picking gelignite at the McKinley-Darragh; Alfred Silvola, blown up while loading holes at the Nipissing; Napolean Taylor, buried by rock at the Nova Scotia.

same luck that fueled the prospectors hopes? Was it the same luck that led the lotteries of Cobalt stocks? One day, through no fault of your own, your luck could give out. You could be blinded by mucking a piece of gelignite. You could be mangled in a cage or buried alive in the ore chute. This was a dreadful luck.

> *You thought that the whole world was mines. Everywhere we looked there were large mines. The street car tracks went right through the McKinley-Darragh mine. The ore cars went overhead from the head-frame to the mill carrying ore. At another mine, black, wooden wire-wrapped pipes carried cyanide to the slime dumps.*
> – Mrs. Bronte Svekers, retired school teacher, 1972

The early operations began with the digging of silver from extremely rich surface veins. Since milling and refining techniques were costly and required a fair degree of technical knowledge, only the richest silver was retrieved. This primitive quarrying method allowed numerous small companies to come into being, companies that would never have got off the ground if shaft sinking and underground development were required.

The ore was hauled out in buckets that swung precariously above the men working below. The thin band of silver was followed tenaciously, creating a narrow, tortuous descent into the earth. Men went at the rock with picks and shovels. They blasted their rounds with drill holes made in the rock with a hand-held bit and a sledgehammer.

Usually these surface veins were only workable to a depth of forty or fifty feet. Then the operation would dry up or money would be reinvested to follow veins that were harder to access. The Meyer vein system on the Nipissing property reflects a common ore pattern of the early camp. On the surface it appeared as a meagre three-quarter-inch barren run of calcite. But down at about a hundred feet, it blossomed with rich silver. Over thirteen million ounces were extracted from this vein alone.

Underground mining required expertise. Even though the shafts in Cobalt were never very deep, there remained a need for experienced engineers and mining draftsmen. Mining experts came from British East Africa and South Africa. Mine managers and captains came in from the copper fields of Colorado, from Butte, Montana, and from Arizona.

As extraction methods became more involved, the companies had to build the proper infrastructure to allow the development to continue. Shafts were sunk and mills built. Timber yards needed to be maintained, blacksmith shops, cookhouses, and even hospital quarters were set up. The mines became a world unto themselves, swallowing up the men of the town in the morning, returning them to surface once the day was done.

The men were lowered down the shaft in an elevator known as a cage. The main thoroughfare in the Coniagas Mine was down the #2 shaft. The headframe above the shaft watched over the town as one of the spires of the many industrial congregations.

It was cold underground. The dank air cut through the oilskins and numbed the toes. What made the cold worse was the water. It sprayed down the sides of the shaft, pumping greater in sections where the water table had been broken. Let the pumps stop and the drifts would slowly fill with this cold, dead water.

The air was never very good. At the best of times it was hard to keep a candle lit and without a candle the darkness was absolute. A man made his way with the drill, the pick, or the blasting rounds by the light of this candle. It sat in a little iron holder worn on a soft hat or stuck in a fissure where they worked. The old-fashioned candles gave way to carbide lamps by around 1910, not out of deference to progress, but because the air in the mines was too weak to sustain the flickering light. There wasn't enough air for a candle, but enough apparently for a man to do a hard ten-hour day.[*]

Very early in the development of Cobalt, the hand-steel drilling of the old packsack miners gave way to the new heavy and thunderously loud pneumatic drills. The miners hated these drills, for they destroyed the ear drums and ravaged the lungs. They called the drills "widowmakers."[†]

Besides the danger of the dust, men had to contend with the poisonous gases that sometimes remained trapped in pockets underground after explosions. Ventilation technology was nonexistent and since few of the mines had vent raises to carry away dead air, trapped gas was a constant threat. Hilda Parcher remembers her father coming home every night soaking wet from working underground. "After blasting," she recalls, "he always had terrible headaches."

Blasting fuses and dynamite caused many accidents. If the dynamite was frozen, the men had to thaw it out over a flame. The unstable quality of dynamite that had put an end to poor John Shannon and countless others became a real issue for the miners and companies of Cobalt. In 1910 the local mine managers were demanding that the government begin implementing quality control of the dynamite brought into the province.

Once the men went down the shaft, they would be let out at the various levels leading to underground roadways. The tunnels were known as drifts. The men walked down the drifts until they came to their work station (known as a stope) where the ore

---

[*]According to some local miners, even in recent years Cobalt miners took it for granted that if they wanted to light a cigarette underground they needed to light an entire book of matches in one go. Only then would there be enough flame to ignite the cigarette.

[†]The dry drills began a long and sad tradition of miners' widows in the north as silicosis established itself as a major illness among mining men. The problem was magnified many times when the mines began to open in the heavy silica-laden gold mines further north. In 1914 the hollow steel drill was introduced in Cobalt and this device greatly lowered the dust levels underground. Some companies, however, saw no reason to invest in these drills unless compensated by the government.

was extracted. To get into a stope you had to climb a ladder up a narrow raise. The stope followed the length and width of the vein of silver. Men worked at the vein from below. They would blast down a section of the roof, climb up on the rubble, and blast out another round until eventually the vein was depleted.

Although the rock in the Cobalt camp tended to be very stable, there was always a danger in the stopes of caveins and rock falls. Rock that was blasted after one shift might still be hanging loose in sections at the beginning of the next shift. The crew entering the stope after a blast had to bang against the roof of the stope with long scaling bars to make sure that all the loose rock was down. If the roof above them remained unstable it had to be secured with timbers while the miners went about the next level in their work.

Men who had come from the big mines out west knew how important it was to make sure that the timbering was done right. If the timbering wasn't perfect, it was the miners who ended up risking the most. W. H. P. Jarvis, in his book *Trails and Tales in Cobalt*, quotes a saying among the mine managers: "Men are cheaper than timbers."

The removal of the ore from the stope was the job of the muckers and the trammers. Mucking was the hard, backbreaking work of shoveling out the tons of loose rock into the ore chute or directly into the ore cars. The trammer had the job of pushing the heavily laden ore up the drift along the narrow set of railway tracks.

My father came to Cobalt in 1904 and along with a lot of other Cornish men went to work for Captain Harris. He was the Cornish captain here and most of the Cornish men went to work for him. My father and his partner were working out in the Nipissing mine and they were tramming over an eighty-foot chute with the ore car when the tramway broke. His partner was killed and my father suffered serious injuries which he never got over. There was no workman's compensation then and he had seven children, with two more on the way.
— Ernie Tressider, retired grocery store owner, 1993

There is very little left today of the wide expanse of operations carried out in Cobalt. Many of the properties have been overgrown with weeds and poplars. At the once-mighty Coniagas Mine, there remains only some broken foundation on a desert of bluish-green sand rising above the hockey arena. On Saturday morning the arena parking lot is full of youngsters hauling their gear from cars for practices and tournaments. On a geological map it still carries the designation of its former glory — Jack Pot City.

CHAPTER TEN

Learning from the School of Life

I was born and raised here in Mileage 104. The stamp mill went day and night. It was very dusty and you could hear the pounding of the ore from far away. If the stamp mill ever stopped in the night, people would wake up and wonder what was going on. The superintendent of the mill was Claude O'Shaughnessy. His wife, Minnie Meredith, used to teach me in school. She was a lovely person and he was very nice, too. They met and were married. They had a large family.

– Ralph Benner, geologist and former Cobalt resident

LEO AND CLAUDE O'SHAUGHNESSY were just boys when they arrived in Cobalt with their family in the autumn of 1913. They had left Enfield, Nova Scotia, on a warm Indian summer day, but arrived in Cobalt under a covering of snow. Winter had arrived. At the station they were met by Captain McLeod and the O'Brien horse and buggy team. McLeod took the family of ten through town to the O'Brien townsite.

As the horses slowly made their way from the station past the jumble of stores on the one side and the impressive workings of the Nipissing Mill on the other, the two brothers stared wide-eyed at the new world they were entering. The farm life was over. The boys would soon join their father as employees of Michael J. O'Brien, the man who personally owned one of the richest mines in the area.

Michael John O'Brien had begun his career as a water boy on the railway, but through tenacity and drive he grew wealthy off the railroads. He was one of the men chosen to lead the building of the railway into northern Ontario. It is not surprising, then, that he was one of the first investors in the Cobalt camp.

By the time the O'Shaughnessy family became part of the O'Brien operation, the mine was well established. As soon as Leo was old enough, he went to work underground earning between a $1.60 and $2.50 for a day that lasted eleven hours on the day shift and thirteen hours on the night shift. Leo remembers how busy the mine site was in those days.

> *The mines were very active. The larger ones were well equipped with various ma-chines to make their own horseshoes, steel parts for machines, for mine cars, cages, dozens of other little things. Any parts to be replaced were made right there. The carpenter was very important in the mine. In those days anything that could be made by wood was made by the carpenter, the decks for the mill, table decks and ladders. Pretty near all the mines had cookeries, dining halls and sleep-ing quarters for the miners. Every meal was a big one and the very best.*

Claude O'Shaughnessy went to work sweeping the floors in the big stamp mill. Built in 1913, the O'Brien stamp mill that overlooked the village of Mileage 104 (just outside Cobalt) had eighty large iron stampers to crush the rock. When ore was brought up from underground it was sent along a trestle to the mill, which crushed the rock into fine powder and separated the silver from impurities. The crushing was carried out by the giant iron shoes that pounded twenty-four hours a day. They had to be specially timed not to fall in tandem or the building would be shaken apart.

The milling processes in Cobalt had primitive beginnings. The first mines only went after ore pure enough to be bagged on the spot and sent to surface. When the rich high-grade ore began to give out, the mines found they had to start mining into lesser grade rock where silver was mixed in with deposits of cobalt, arsenic, iron, and waste rock. The ore was then crushed and poured over screens so valuable rock could be picked out by hand. But soon it became clear that a great deal of valuable silver was being tossed out with the waste. In 1907, the first gravity mill was introduced in Cobalt. After the ore had been crushed to a fine powder it was run through a water table that stirred the rocks and created a coating of bubbles. The valuable minerals became at-tached to the bubbles and were skimmed off, while the rest was either tossed out as waste or sent back for further refining.[*]

In 1908 the Buffalo Mine began experimenting with adding cyanide to the water mixture to chemically separate the silver. Cyanide and mercury treatment techniques greatly increased the recovery of silver, but it resulted in an environmental disaster as the companies began dumping the toxic residue in lakes and streams around Cobalt. Over the years the heavier elements have settled, but the eerie green beaches of Cobalt still testify to the desolation brought about by this toxic process.

---

[*]Local prospector John Gore states that this extraction process was started during the California Gold Rush, when the women doing the laundry noticed that gold flakes on the men's clothes stuck to the bub-bles while the resin and grime fell to the bottom of the tub.

*All the kids who lived in 104 played at Cross Lake. It was where we spent our sum-
mer holidays. Cross Lake was full of tailings and you'd see cows floating around
in it dead. They used to stray down by the water and drink from it. The cyanide
would kill them and you'd see them floating in the water.*
  – Ralph Benner

Servicing the power requirements of so many mining and milling operations became
a pressing problem. Mine managers were desperately searching for an alternative to
the trainloads of coal that had to be hauled up continually from Pennsylvania. The
cost of running a drill machine was as high as $250 a month. At that time, hydroelec-
tric power was still in its infancy. The pressure to create cheaper fuel sources for the
mines helped move Ontario towards massive hydro expansion.

   Charles Taylor arrived at this time in Cobalt, hoping to convince the local mine
owners to back his theory of creating a new alternative to fossil fuels. His design was
brilliant in its simplicity. At the Ragged Chutes Falls, Taylor supervised the sinking of
a shaft that would draw in the cascading waters of the Montreal River during its thou-
sand-foot plunge into Lake Temiskaming. The shaft allowed the water to suck down
air with it in its torrent, creating a vacuum effect. When the water reached bottom it
was diverted and the air pushed through a pipe, which produced more than a hundred
pounds per square inch of pressure through countless miles of iron pipe that ran from
the Ragged Chutes to all the outlying mine sites. It provided a steady and cheap source
of energy for the mines and mills of the whole area. "How long will your plant run?"
the mine managers asked Taylor when he approached them with his idea. "Perhaps
forever," he replied.

   In addition to the Ragged Chutes, Hydro plants at Hound Chutes and at the Mati-
bitchuwan River helped in the expansion of the Cobalt mills, but even so there
weren't sufficient power reserves to make the building of refineries economical in the
area.* High-grade silver ore could be processed locally, but the lesser grade ores,
tainted with high levels of arsenic and cobalt, had to be shipped out to refineries at
Deloro and Thorold in southern Ontario, or to New Jersey.

   The rush to find cheaper and easier methods of extracting minerals turned Cobalt
into a huge, dirty laboratory. Metallurgists from all over the world were brought in. For
a young man like Claude O'Shaughnessy, it was an exciting time and a once-in-a-
lifetime chance to get a hands-on education. Limen McEwan, the mill superintendent,

---

*The need to assure adequate hydro power was a lesson obviously learned by men like the Timmins
brothers, who made sure that in the new gold camp of the Porcupine, the hydro potential along the
Mattagami and Abitibi rivers would be utilized. Ontario's leap into the world of megahydroelectric projects was greatly influenced by the need to provide energy for the expanding mining operations of Cobalt,
Timmins, and Sudbury.

saw that O'Shaughnessy was a quick study. He took the young lad under his wing and began teaching him the milling process. The boy paid close attention and was soon moved into the assay lab where the final heating and refining of silver was done. There he learnt the chemical processes that were needed to determine silver values and to judge mineral grades. When Limen McEwan died in the late 1920s, Claude O'Shaughnessy was chosen to take his place as mill superintendent. He moved his family into the superintendent's house at the back of the mill and lived there for almost forty years.

He became an integral part of the operations of the O'Brien Mining Company. When the O'Brien owners decided to close up their operations in Cobalt, Claude O'Shaughnessy took control of the mill himself and for decades did custom work for the small operations still going in the area. The mill had numerous different names during its existence, but most folks simply referred to it as the O'Shaughnessy Mill.

The old stamp mill loomed over the little village of Mileage 104 for so long that it became part of the identity of the people who lived there. In the life of a mining town, the mines and mill sites hold a particular power over the people of the place. When the O'Shaughnessy Mill burnt in 1956, part of the living memory of the town burnt with it.

I remember when the O'Brien Mill burned down. That was the last stamp mill in the camp. Jeez, those stamps were noisy. After the mill burnt the stamps fell down. The people living in 104 couldn't sleep after the mill burnt down, they were so used to the sound.

    – Marvin Armstrong, retired diamond driller, 1993

CHAPTER ELEVEN

The Prince Finally Comes

I know now what it means when your muscles, your vocal chords, your memory box, start to age. You don't just wake up in the morning and decide that you're going to get old. The desires that you have wither, decay, and leave you. It comes for me now and it will come for you tomorrow. It comes to us all. It is in man and that is why we fight so hard.

– Bob Carlin, labour activist , 1991

T HE DAY the Prince of Wales came was cold and gray. He arrived in Cobalt in 1919 to visit the heralded mining sensation of the empire. Silver Street was a sea of Union Jacks and loyal subjects. But flags and crowds could not throw off the dismal cloak of industrial grime that hung over the town. It was relentless. The town had just come through a devastating influenza epidemic. Labour unrest was boiling over. Some of the silver mines had begun to close. The Prince had come, but he was too late. Cobalt's gown was returning to rags.

Prince Edward descended from the train and took the tour in the convertible car past the smiling faces looking out from the Royal Exchange Building. He crossed the Coniagas #4 shaft in the heart of the downtown with the mounds of waste rock behind it, and was presented at the buildings of the main Coniagas complex. The Prince had seen all that Cobalt had to offer and shrugged it off: "Ah, it's a gray, wee town."

Gertrude Underwood was a young woman of twenty-one at the time of the visit. "I think the actual downfall of Cobalt was when the Prince of Wales came. He was a young man then. The day dawned gray and weary, and it never changed. Colonel Rodgers took him to the Coniagas and even the mine looked cold and gray. I think after this visit most of the money was pulled out of Cobalt."

Cobalt in 1919 wasn't any more gray or dismal than usual, but the glamour had vanished. The decline had begun. Silver reserves were being rapidly depleted and new ones were not being found. The high profits that had sustained the camp through the war were deceiving; most of the profits were due to better milling techniques, not new discoveries. Mine owners had known in 1912 that the reserves of silver wouldn't last. Underground conditions were deteriorating and the machinery barely maintained. Many people assumed that once the war was over life would return to normal, but the big money was pulling up stakes for the new promised land further north.

If there hadn't been a war, the collapse of Cobalt would have been evident much sooner.[*] It had really begun with the discovery of massive gold deposits in the Porcupine and Kirkland Lake area. The rise of the Porcupine was delayed by a devastating bush fire in 1911 that wiped out the camp and all the mine workings. But the delay was fleeting. Townsites were quickly rebuilt and the money was pouring in to support large-scale gold exploration. It was money from Cobalt.[†]

"The best old town" was living on borrowed time. And yet, the deterioration was overshadowed by a much larger crisis in the western world. The war had ruined the economies of Europe. Inflation and unemployment were everywhere. The crisis was exacerbated by the return of thousands of soldiers who believed that their sacrifice in Europe should be rewarded by jobs. In Russia, workers had overthrown the Czar. In Germany, veteran soldiers were fighting pitched gun battles in the streets, as socialists and right-wing gangs fought for control of the country.

In western Canada this discontent led to the rising power of the One Big Union — a belief that if workers threw their lot in with one all-encompassing union, they could wage a general strike that would bring capitalism to its knees. The result was the famous Winnipeg General Strike of 1919. In eastern Canada, the call to leave the old unions and join the One Big Union (OBU) fell pretty much on deaf ears. But in the mining camps of northern Ontario, the prospect of a more militant labour presence fell on fertile ground. The mining camps had always had small but vocal anarcho-syndicalist and communist sympathizers.

In Cobalt, the One Big Union was promoted by Jim Cluny, an underground miner. Cluny publicly accused Big Jim McGuire, a surface man, of not having the underground miners' interests at heart. Cluny believed that the union structure (now reaffiliated as the Mine Mill and Smelter Workers) had ceased being the voice of the

---

[*]In 1916, silver mines almost went out on a general strike in Cobalt. According to historian Brian Hogan, this strike was only averted by the intervention of the British Treasury, which was dependent on silver bullion. Fearing it would damage their fragile war-time economy, the British Treasury put pressure on Prime Minister Borden to induce the mine managers to come to terms.

[†]Mine owners had known in 1912 that the reserves of silver wouldn't last. Although this wasn't public knowledge, it was becoming obvious that they hadn't been putting any money into their Cobalt operation for some years.

workers and that the miners should throw in their lot with the OBU. This internal strife was also tearing apart the Locals in Timmins and Kirkland Lake.

Against this background of world-wide labour unrest and a threatening fissure in the Canadian trade-union movement, the Cobalt Miners' Union submitted a list of demands to the Temiskaming Managers' Association on June 2, 1919. Their list of demands were moderate. They asked for a Sabbath day of rest. There was anger at how the managers controlled the local hospital, which was paid for out of workers' wages.[*] The issue of land tenure remained unresolved, and workers knew that the threat of eviction could always be used against anyone who became too vocal in the union. But it was the final two issues that were the most contentious—an increase in wages due to spiralling inflation and the recognition of the right to collective bargaining. The mine owners refused to even acknowledge the union's existence.[†] A strike vote was held the following week and passed by a margin of eleven hundred to two hundred.

Once again the papers filled with the spectre of the Red menace. *Saturday Night* magazine led the parade by declaring that the "Banner of Bolshevism waves over Cobalt." The spectre of impending violence was a creation of journalistic whimsy, but nonetheless the camp was cleared of dynamite. Additional police were called in.

By this time the wives of the miners had organized a Ladies Auxiliary. Joined by single female sympathizers, they entered the fray. Maude Groom recounts a spirited intervention of a ladies auxiliary whose main task was to patrol the streets on the lookout for scabs. Miss Katherine Sampson, Mrs. Dan Kearney, and Geraldine McCrank managed to stop one potential scab who was sneaking up the railway line in search of work.

> *They grabbed him and put a woman's apron on him, then the three of them paraded him down to Cobalt. They marched him down Lang Street to the Union office. As they led him along, the three young women scolded him soundly.*
>
> *"Young fellow," chided Mrs. Kearney in her motherly way, "I know you don't realize what you are doing. We are all in this together, fighting for human rights. If we falter now, we lose what ground we've made. We could easily land back into slavery again."*

---

[*]The hospital had a policy of only treating workers, not their dependents. During the influenza epidemic of the previous year, many women and children were forced to take the five-mile journey to Haileybury. Miners who lost children from the epidemic or resulting pneumonia blamed the hard-line policy of the hospital, which was run by the Managers' Association.

[†]The hardline approach adopted by the Mine Managers' Association to workers demands may have been due to the fact that most companies were owned by distant and American owners. The local managers who realized the conditions in the camp were given little leeway to accommodate any increase to the employees.

Negotiations concerning the strike were complicated by another rift in the miners' ranks, created by the presence of the Great War Veterans Association. The distrust between labour and the veterans was common in all the countries that had taken part in the war. Some vets resented the "foreigners" who remained at home with well-paying jobs while they were fighting in France. The companies were quick to play up the "loyalty" of the veterans and the "Bolshevik" plottings of the union.

Initially the veterans had sided with the union, boasting they would be willing to stay out on strike all winter if need be, convinced they could survive the season by bagging game with their Luger pistols smuggled home from the front. But by the fourth week of the strike, hardships were increasing. Many of the veterans in particular were caught financially ill-prepared for a strike. Dan Hellens remembers a union protest outside his father's house when his father sided with other veterans in crossing the picket lines. His father pulled out a gun, Hellens states, and threatened to kill the strikers if they didn't get off his property.

For union men like Jim McGuire, the struggle to overcome ethnic bitterness had been a fundamental and unalterable tenet of the union. A story told by Bob Carlin underlines McGuire's belief in the notion that "an injury to one is an injury to all."

The story goes that McGuire was in the chair at a Union meeting and the words "Bohunk," "Flathead," "Hunky" came up four or five times. And McGuire said, "I don't like those terms Flathead, Meathead, Bohunk." And so they passed a motion striking those words. Then this big Swedish fellow gets up. Now he and McGuire were thought of as the two best men in the union, indeed in all of Cobalt, to walk around rather than try and walk through. They were tough men. "Well," said the Swede, "'I didn't make any money last week , but then how can you make any money if the guy you've got on the other end of the machine doesn't know what it's all about. My helper, a Polish Bohunk, doesn't know anything about drilling." McGuire said, "Did you not hear the reading of the minutes? That word was brought up and it was rejected out of hand and any further use of it in this hall will demand an apology to the person affected. If not, he will be asked to leave the hall immediately." "Well," said the Swede, "'I'd like to see the man who would expel me from this meeting." He then used the offending word again. McGuire walked over to the door and he looked back and signed for the big fellow to follow.

McGuire turned to him and said, "Take your coat off." The big fellow replied, "Oh, I don't think I need to take my coat off to you, McGuire." McGuire said, "Have it as you will. Any blood to be spilled will be your blood, not mine." He squared up just ready to strike when the big fellow grabbed his hand and started to shake his hand. He said, "McGuire, I'm not backing down because I'm afraid of you. You're right. You're 100 percent right as you always are." So they came into the hall their arms linked and the big fellow was the first one to speak. He said, "If I ever hear any of you using the words Bohunk, or Flathead, or Meathead, in here or on Union property, I'll see that McGuire kicks the crap out of you, and if he doesn't, I'll kick the crap out of you."

The strike lasted six weeks. The miners' families had existed through that time with no income, and with the threat of winter approaching, the union felt it was important to try and broach an agreement. The job of selling the settlement to the workers fell to Jim McGuire. The failure of the strike, coupled with pressure for a more radical stand, was too much for the Cobalt local. Jim Cluny and the OBU supporters accused McGuire of selling them out, and led a breakaway from the Mine Mill leadership in Denver. Bob Carlin remembers how devastated McGuire was by this rejection, "Big Jim got a very dirty break. The miners felt that when the strike ended he had sold them out. You might say that his life was ended after the strike."

The sun was setting on the short-lived glory of Cobalt. As the union broke apart in acrimony and recriminations, the silver mines began to close. For years the companies had existed on bloated profits because they were mining only the high-grade deposits and ignoring the lower-grade ore. Now that the rich shallow beds of high-grade were disappearing, the cost of going after the low-grade was becoming prohibitive. The mines began to close. The exodus up to Timmins and Kirkland Lake became a stampede.

Carlin moved on with the rest of the miners. But he had been touched by the dreams of Big Jim McGuire. There was a better world out there waiting to be born, a better way of treating people and better way of being treated. This became the life-long mission of Bob Carlin.* But there were rough years ahead. Within two years of taking over the mine locals of Timmins, Cobalt, and Kirkland Lake, the OBU fell apart under government persecution and internal disorganization. The unions disappeared in the north for the better part of twenty years. When they resurfaced in Kirkland Lake during the bitter strike of 1941, Carlin was there. And so was McGuire.

When we were on the big organizing drive towards the Kirkland Lake strike I went after Jim McGuire to sign a card. In the old days you couldn't dodge him if he was after you to join the union, but when I met him in Kirkland he seemed reluctant to join the fight. I asked if he had changed his mind. "Oh no," he said, "the working people deserve a piece of the wealth. We want a more equitable distribution of the wealth of the world between the people who produce the wealth. But I'm a

---

*Bob Carlin became one of the most important labour activists in the history of the north. In 1944 he led the organizing drive against INCO and Falconbridge in Sudbury. He was then elected as a socialist member to the Legislature. During the struggle between Mine Mill and the United Steelworkers, Bob Carlin joined Steel as a staff rep.

little bit too old to change things." Now God help the person who said that to him when he was a young organizer. I said, "Jimmy, do you remember a young fella who once said if you're not too old or too young to work in the mine, then you're not too old or too young to join the union." "Oh," he says, "you've got a good memory. Give me a card."

Bob Carlin was over ninety when he was interviewed for this book. He was living in an old folks' home that had once been the manager's estate of the rich Kerr-Addison Mine in Virginiatown, Ontario. The irony wasn't lost on him. From a quick glance he seemed like just one of the countless elders who had been shelved by a busy world. All the heroes and characters of the old Cobalt Camp were dead. And yet the great struggle remained.

I see how far we have come over the last eighty years in killing people, in planning for killing people and the destruction of people's property. What have the working people been doing all that time? There are many working people with high wages, and there's nothing wrong with that, this is what we fought for, but they didn't develop high ideals. What we have now is only a shadow of the spirit we had yesterday. It makes me think of the kind of union men we had in Cobalt, Salt Lake City, and Butte, Montana, where every time you'd meet these people they radiated something that said, "The fight is here and I'll fight to the very, very end of it." It's like Old Jim you know, they started little dreams. But so many of them took it with them. When you see that spark in someone—watch them.

2

Within Living Memory

T HE CLASSROOMS of Saint Patrick's school look out over the rusted headframe of the Right of Way Mine and the barren hills and slime dumps of the old Nipissing properties.

"There used to be big veins of silver here and that is why there are big holes up in the hills now," says a girl pointing to the open cuts.

Where did the silver go?

A young fellow with a Los Angeles Kings sweatshirt excitedly puts up his hand. "It was in a train," he explains, "and the train tripped into the lake and that's where all the silver went."

This sets off a furious debate.

"They didn't have trains in the olden days."

"Yes they did."

"No they didn't."

What else might have happened to the silver?

"They took all the money and left."

Who did?

"The Yankees took it."

Where did it go?

"Away."

"To Toronto."

Then what happened?

"They tried looking for more, but there was none left."

– The history of Cobalt according to the grade five students of Saint Patrick's School, Cobalt, Ontario, March 30, 1993.

CHAPTER TWELVE

The Friendless Finn

_____

I remember my Daddy saying that Cobalt, like a lot of little mining towns, was a place that wasn't meant to stay. It was meant to be mined and left. Buildings were put up dishevelled and without any order, because the thinking was that when it was mined out people would move on to the next town. And yet, the mines died and the people are still there.

– Laura Landers, local artist, 1991

O N A LAZY DAY in June 1988, the highway in front of John Damiani's furniture store started to open up. A couple of local children noticed the small hole in the road and began tossing rocks down it. The rocks seemed to take forever to hit bottom. A public works crew quickly sent to repair the road realized that this was no ordinary pothole; Cobalt's main thoroughfare was being devoured by a collapsing mine stope. Dump trucks were sent to backfill, but as the days went on, the efforts were in vain. The "world's largest pothole" had an insatiable appetite.

Emergency sonar cameras were brought in to explore the bowels of Cobalt. The results were unsettling. As it turned out, the collapsing roadway was no isolated phenomenon. In fact, the whole south end of town was honeycombed with shafts, drifts, and caverns. Some came perilously close to surface. It was a nasty reminder of the chaos that had occurred back in the days of silver fever.

Armand Coté lives across from the spot where the highway caved in. Until his retirement in 1990, he supervised the reopening of numerous old mining properties in Cobalt. Working as the area superintendent for Agnico-Eagle Mines, Coté supervised the dewatering of old shafts. Once the shafts were clear, they began exploring neglected drifts for undiscovered silver.

His house is on the property that once belonged to the Mining Corporation of Canada. The large double garage in his backyard was the hoist room for one of the shafts. Nearby, Damiani's Furniture sits directly on top of this shaft. From the window in Coté's living room you can see the Townsite headframe #1. Its tall, rusted, and bent body is a familiar symbol for anyone driving into Cobalt. The land surrounding the head-frame is slowly beginning to cave in and extensive work has gone into stabilizing its base.

One of the most dangerous sections of ground was just a stone's throw from the Coté house. The front lawn of the old folks' home sits on top of the old City of Cobalt Mine shaft and the main workings of the mine are right under the apartments. A house further up Galena Street had to be torn down in the early 1990s after the resident noticed that her yard also had a ravenous appetite for topsoil. It turned out that her property was being sucked slowly down the shaft of the Nancy Helen Mine.

On the hill rising up Galena Street, huge canyons and crevices lurk in behind sedate residential dwellings. At times it seems that the only thing holding back these mighty gorges is a thin ribbon of pavement. In 1992 the bomb squad had to be called into this neighbourhood after two boys dragged home a box they found in a part of the old Buffalo Mine. Their haul of interesting loot turned out to be a case of very unstable dynamite.

Giant potholes and occasional dynamite scares are nothing new in Cobalt. It is something that the generations growing up in the years after the boom have grown used to. It is part of the hazards of living on the old battlefields of silver.

When the mines began to close in the early 1920s, the closure laws that safeguard mine closures today were nonexistent . The companies just walked away. They left Cobalt littered with abandoned mine operations and waste dumps. The lakes and waterways of the area were choked with tailings—many of them toxic. The hills had been stripped of vegetation and left with undermined earth. The silver barons had little time for long goodbyes.

This was the world Armand Coté was born into. At the time of his birth in 1921, the Mining Corporation of Canada had emerged as one of the three major employers in town. As smaller mines closed, Mining Corporation bought them up and soon they were controlling all the workings on the south side of town. In all its workings, the Mining Corporation employed about 190 men in the 1920s. Across the lake, the Nipissing Mine was still making great strides, with 250 men working. Just a little further north, the O'Brien Mine had emerged as the other solid employer in the camp. It worked its holdings at Cross Lake, on the O'Brien property and in the Violet shaft. Employing about 190 men, the O'Brien would survive the longest[*] of the original companies.

For the remaining mines, the 1920s marked the end of the road. In 1924 the mighty Coniagas closed up. At the LaRose Mine, a cavein underneath the train tracks flooded much of the workings; the mine limped along until its demise in 1927. This was the same year that saw the closing of the McKinley-Darragh Mine, which had come into the decade employing about a hundred men. The Silver Queen was still in operation in 1921, but two of its three levels were flooded. It would soon follow the Right of Way,

---

[*]In 1939, M. J. O'Brien sold off the mine, the foundry, and the mill to interested local parties.

the Temiskaming, the Trethewey, the Beaver, and the Hudson Bay, which had shut down altogether. Gone like chaff were the countless companies that had been created to drum up interest in the Cobalt camp.

For years the mines at Kerr Lake had feasted on the richest veins of the camp. The high-grade Carson vein ran 286 feet long and 156 feet deep. It was the richest silver vein ever found (producing nine million ounces of silver). In 1920, with faltering production, the Crown Reserve tried deep drilling, hoping to find a second layer of riches in the depths below. There was nothing to be had. With only a measly 1,121 ounces of silver to show for 1921, it closed along with the other Kerr Lake operations. The community of Kerr Lake was swallowed by the bush.

The sudden collapse of the local industry created a unique situation in Cobalt. Many of the workings were still intact and the surface buildings standing. The dumps were often still full of good ore that had been passed over when only high-grade was desired. In the community there remained experienced mining men who knew the intimate workings of these properties. It didn't take too long before enterprising individuals began leasing the sites and trying their hand at running the mines themselves.

Armand Coté got his first experience underground on one of these leasing crews: "I first started underground when I was seventeen. My father was a lumberjack. He took a lease on the old Silver Cliff Mine with his brother-in-law. We went in and worked the mine for awhile. You couldn't make any money leasing. We weren't there very long."

It is hard to imagine today the circumstances that made the work of the leasers possible. Mining today is a highly capital-intensive operation. It requires millions of dollars of investment and is intensely regulated. But in the Cobalt of the 1920s, it was still relatively easy for five or six men to go into an old mine and try their hand at picking the last meat off the bones. These were often small, family-run operations. Coté looks upon the simplicity that surrounded the leasing operations as if it were from a different world.

Nowadays it would be very difficult to lease a mine and get it into operation because of the prohibitive cost of buying compressors and other equipment. Years ago, the compressed air was supplied by Hydro and charged monthly for the amount of air consumed. But the air plant at Ragged Chutes has been dismantled and all the pipes to the mines removed. You'd never be able to do something like that now, to just go in and operate a mine. You'd never have the money to get started.

The repercussions of the early leasers operations are still evident today. Since many of these were rag-tag operations, issues of structural engineering weren't often considered. If there was silver left in the support pillars they thought nothing of blasting it out. The damage was cumulative. Many properties were leased again and again by different crews. John Gore, a life-long resident, believes that few leasers would have realized the long-term implications of these scavenging operations.

> *The leasers were good practical men, but they were not professional engineers. They worked in places where men wouldn't work today and took chances and so you have the caveins and such that you have today. In those days the heaviest load you would get on a road would be maybe one or two tons. Most travelling was still horse and wagons. When the leasers went after the ore that was left in the pillars underground, they went closer to the surface than they should have. But even so, who would have thought that you'd someday have transports of sixty tons going through on the roads.*

For children growing up in the shadow of the boom, the once-rich mines still offered promise. Children earned spending money by picking silver and cobalt ore from the dumps. They brought their haul in little buckets to the leasers who paid them for what they found. Ralph Benner (who outlined the famous Denison ore body) got his first lessons in geology while trying to raise enough money to go to the picture shows. John Gore explains how the waste dumps were worked:

> *We'd go out after a rain because the cobalt and metallics would shine through and we'd go pick it up trying to get enough money to go to the show. There's an intelligent system to picking at the dumps. We learnt it from the older people who brought us out. You'd find ore in the dumps just like you would a vein, because of the time it was brought out and dumped. You would pick around the dumps, prospect if you will, until you came to where there was cobalt. You got paid ten cents a pound for high-grade, that is silver you could feel in your hand. We were probably ten years old then.*

Children who grew up in the years following the boom remember Cobalt as still being a very vital and interesting community. The streetcars were still running and downtown business, although a shadow of the peak years, remained respectable. The years of helter-skelter development had, however, begun to take its toll. The town's sidewalks were in a terrible condition. The sidewalk below the Cobalt Reduction Plant was in a state of poor repair owing to the continual falling of rocks from the plant. Other sidewalks were being damaged because heavy wagons and mining trucks seemed to prefer driving over the sidewalks because they were better maintained than the roads. The town had to draft a by-law prohibiting driving on sidewalks. Enforcement, however, was another matter.

Then, of course, there were the problems posed by the abandoned mine workings. In one case, the town tried unsuccessfully in 1923 to force the Aladdin Mining Company to deal with the hazards created by their Earle Street shaft. The company ignored their requests and the mining inspector had to be brought in.

With the companies shirking responsibility for the infrastructure problems plaguing Cobalt, the burden fell onto municipal shoulders. Lacking an adequate tax base, however, the town was unable to improve conditions. The council notes for the decade reveal a town reeling from economic hardship. Mrs. Salimen approached council saying she could not afford the taxes on her LaRose Street home. Her husband was dead and her daughter had only occasional work. Mrs. McKenzie of Earle Street asked to be exempted from her 1923 taxes. She was a widow with two children. Another widow, Mrs. Boisvenue, could not afford her taxes. Neither could Mrs. Bernachia, a widow with three children. Mrs. Smith, widowed with two small children, requested tax exemption.

Perhaps one of the most poignant cases to come before the Town Council was the case of Mr. Oscar Kivi. Mr. Kivi had come before the town in July of 1923, suffering from tuberculosis and unable to look after himself. *The North Bay Nugget* dubbed him "the Friendless Finn":

> *Unable to understand the discussion which revolved about his own person a few feet away from where he sat and obviously suffering from a dread disease, an apparently friendless Finn waited patiently while the Cobalt Town Council wrestled with the problem his condition created. Compatriots stated that the man had lost his health while working in the mines and was now consumptive, and they thought that the town should look after the sufferer who, from time to time, gave evidence of his malady. It appeared that the Finn had been cared for by his fellow countrymen and women, but the family with whom he had been living was unable to care for him any longer. He had been in good physical health when he came to Canada in 1914 and "the Finnish people and taxpayers" were of the opinion that, since the man had lost his health while working in the mines, the onus of providing for him rested upon the municipality. The man had slept outside the night previous.*

What had brought Mr. Kivi to Cobalt? Was it the dreams of the silver rush or did he come simply because there was work to be had? After only six years of working in the mines of Cobalt, his health was destroyed and now he was friendless in a town too poor to pay for his upkeep. The Town Council listened to the plea for help and voted to send him to the Toronto Free Hospital for Consumptives. When the hospital in Toronto finally contacted the town requesting that they cover his expenses, including his burial should it become necessary, the town washed its hands of poor Mr. Kivi. "He's not our responsibility," they said, "because he lived and worked in one of the unorganized townships." Apparently Oscar Kivi was friendless to the end.

CHAPTER THIRTEEN

A Playground
Like No Other

———————

I'll tell you one thing, Cobalt was the greatest place in the world to raise children. We didn't know it then, but looking at it today, and through the eyes of my own grandchildren, I realize that we had a Disneyland of our own. We had a playground here like nobody has. The Buffalo Mine was a particularly wonderful place to play. It had a long cement tunnel that ran from the upper parts of the mill down to where the old tables used to be. There were parts of the ball mills and rod mills still there. We had miles of pipe line to run along. It came from Ragged Chutes and you could run on it and it had a musical sound to it, from the different ways of running. Some kids took those pipes right across the open cuts but I never did because I didn't have the nerve. I recall stories of kids going underground and riding on rafts but I never did anything like that.

– John Gore, retired mill-worker, 1991

THROUGH THE EYES of a boy, it was magic. Everywhere he turned there were winding trails through deep forests, streams to be forded, and deep canyons to be braved. Every clearing boasted a crusader castle with turrets and towers, every cliff had a towering fort. Caves challenged the fainthearted and deep underground passages beckoned the brave. One by one, the old properties were becoming the domain of the children. A generation was growing up that had no memory of the days when these concrete ruins hummed with life. The children renamed these sites and infused them with their own myths and magic. Like waifs at the front line, they played in places that were dangerous and threatening. Countless children, upon reaching adulthood, would think back, shake their heads, and say, "I'm surprised no one was ever killed."

John Gore grew up on the Coniagas property. He remembers watching the leasers blasting away in the old Coniagas workings and then imitating them in play. In Cobalt it was all too easy to blur the line between playground and worksite.

> *In those days, we used to play blasting. The leasers were working the old Conia-*
> *gas and you'd often hear the men yell "fire" when they were going to blast. I was*
> *with a chum of mine and we went over to the Hudson Bay Mine and we got into*
> *the powder magazine. The mine was closed up and deserted but there was still dy-*
> *namite. We didn't break in, the door was open. We took the dynamite and we lit a*
> *fire and ran and hid in the bush where we were yelling "fire." My uncle was com-*
> *ing down the hill and he said, "What are you doing?" I said, "We're blasting."*
> *"Oh ya, " he says and then went a little ways and stopped. "What are you using?"*
> *"Dynamite." He asked where we got it and I said, "at the Hudson Bay Mine." My*
> *God, his face went about fifteen different colours. Old dynamite is very danger-*
> *ous. He managed to put the fire out and he told us that if it was going to blow, it*
> *would have blown as soon as we put it on the flame. We were lucky. All we got was*
> *a good reprimand.*

The 1930s was a tough decade to come of age. The pressures on communities were enormous. Entire families were destitute and some resorted to begging door-to-door for food. At the edges of many northern towns, "jungles" of the unemployed grew up. When these men got desperate, or the authorities got nervous, battles ensued. In Timmins, Cochrane, Sudbury, and Sault Ste. Marie, there were incidents on the streets between the demonstrating unemployed and the local police. Fire hoses and batons were used to keep the smoldering anger of a sidelined generation in check.

Taffy Davis led an angry mob from North Cobalt to the Township of Bucke to demand relief. The township had installed steel bars over the clerk's wicket in the office because there were fears that farmers who were losing their properties might become violent with town officials. The mob of unemployed youths overturned the relief officer's car and the clerk quickly acceded to their demands for relief. According to Maude Groom, the jubilant mob chanted on their way home:

> "Taffy was a Welshman,
> Taffy had a beef;
> Taffy stormed the Township
> and got us all relief."

Many of the families survived the depression because of the management skills of the women. The men spent their days in the fruitless search for work while the women were left to find ways to put food on the table and keep their children clothed. John Gore remembers how difficult this struggle was: "You can talk about the men, but there is no comparison when you talk of the women. The man, he could go away for the day, but the woman was at home. What was she going to cook? Snowballs? She had a family with little children, how was she going to dress them so they could go to school in the morning?"

M. J. Scully arrived with his family in Cobalt in 1931 with the meagre savings they had brought from the nearby community of Silver Centre. He remembers the efforts his mother made to keep the family afloat: "It was pretty scratchy. We survived because of my mother. When we lived in the bush and there was nothing to spend money on, she saved it. When the depression came she was able to dig into the savings. They were too proud to take relief. There were relief services, but you had to be awfully hard up to take it, because people were proud. We never went on relief, but it came pretty darn close."

The Scully family had been part of the big migration of Ottawa Valley families who came looking for work in the mines of northern Ontario. The farms held little promise for the young people of the Valley. Many of the young men left. "They either went to the car factories of Windsor-Detroit or to the mines of northern Ontario," M. J. Scully recalls. His father found work at the Keeley Mine in Silver Centre. In the 1920s Silver Centre was a community that had already bloomed once and died. In the years before the war, this little mining enclave, twenty miles south of Cobalt, thrived when a few extremely high-grade veins of silver were discovered down in the Lorraine Valley. These mines didn't last, but at the start of the 1920s Silver Centre was given a second chance. It flourished for a time on the strength of mines like the Keeley and the Frontier. The depression sounded the death knell for the town of Silver Centre. The price of silver fell and the mines closed. Within a few short years there would be nothing left of the town at all.

> I guess I'm a bit sentimental when I go back to Silver Centre. There's nothing there now at all. When I go there, I don't feel any sadness, just a sense of wonder about how all this works into the scheme of things. At times I've thought of that dinky little mining camp in Silver Centre and how life goes that it mushroomed, prospered, and died all in ten years. And yet it is so significant to me. My father worked there; my mother and my brothers were all there. To think of all the great people who were there, how they have gone on, prospered and made their lives elsewhere. It always struck me how insignificant the place and the situation is, but that it's the people who count. Goodness and holiness will come in that place as well as any other. It is not the mine or the surroundings that are important, it is the people.

M. J. Scully's father tried as best he could to find work in the Cobalt camp, but often it was just short spells working for leasers, followed by long periods of unemployment. In 1937 he found work out at the Miller Lake O'Brien Mine in Gowganda. While the pay wasn't very good and he had to live out in a bush camp, it made the difference be-tween destitution and survival.*

In these years, even children had a part in the family economy. One of the best ways for a youngster to earn a bit of money was down at the Farmers' Market. Every Saturday morning farmers came down from Earlton and New Liskeard to sell vegeta-bles and meat in Cobalt. They came down on the train in the summer. In the winter, great sleighs crossed over the lake from Quebec. Since nobody owned cars, enterpris-ing youngsters had a perfect opportunity to pick up some extra earnings. The children lined the ramp leading down to the railway tracks with their little wagons trying to pass themselves off as miniature taxis.

"We'd line up like taxi drivers all the way to the top of the hill," recalls Joe Malick, "and when a woman would come out with her meat and potatoes we'd shout 'transfer, transfer, lady', and off we'd go. You might run to her house all the way over in French-town or over to Nickel Street. Out of this you might get five cents, the price of a show."

In the summer, entire families headed out to pick blueberries. The blueberry sea-son was "how you put shoes on the children to go to school in the fall," recalls John Gore. It was a big business. "Trucks would come down full of blueberries," says Ernie Tressider, "and drop them at the railway station. It used to be as busy as hell tagging and shipping them to Toronto. I think they were getting fifty cents for a six-quart basket and seventy-five cents for eleven quarts." Boxcar loads of the berries left the train sta-tion at the end of the summer.

People survived on the strong communal bonds that transformed neighbourhoods into large rambling families. "There were some wonderful people here," recalls John Gore. "They used to say that if you started up on Lang Street, by the time you got to the Square you could borrow fifty dollars in nickels and dimes, and this was at a time when twenty-five cents was a lot."

The children who came of age in the depression were born in a struggle to survive and learned very early on that every effort counts. Perhaps this is what underlines the resentment many of the older people in town feel towards the latest victims of the lat-est mining recession. They point to the blueberry fields that are overgrown with ne-glect. Often it is only the old people who go out to pick from the summer bounty. They believe the younger generation has lost the important survival skills that the de-pression children grew up with.

John Gore fears the loss of these skills is debilitating.

Everyone back then had a garden. They had beautiful gardens. Today you have too many lawns and painted things. People want the wrappings. It worries me. It

---

*In 1950, when M. J. Scully was leaving Cobalt to enter the seminary, his father was crushed between the timber and the cage at the Beaver-Temiskaming Mine.

frightens me. Every spring I go up to my cottage and I plant potatoes. Now I could buy them a lot cheaper, but I want to keep the ground up. How do I know what things will be like next year? I always say to my son, "You have to remember how to grow a potato."

MISSING THE TRAIN

Fred LaRose and the legendary fox of Cobalt lore.
Porcupine Mine owners pass by on the train.

GENESIS

Scenes from early Cobalt: A miner carries out rich silver ore in a wheel-barrow.

PRIM AND PROPER

Early Cobalt boarding house above a group at the Buffalo Mine entrance.

TEA TIME

Ladies having tea, superimposed on a graveyard.
Lower right, Georgie Church, long-time resident.

AWESTRUCK

A couple visiting Cobalt in 1910, superimposed on the first house in Cobalt.
Joe Crutch, a character from the past, smiles from the window.

THE KOBOLD AND THE PHOENIX

A train derailment is joined with an image of the fire of 1909.
Fred LaRose (foreground) and an early silver miner make an appearance.

THE LOTTERY

A modern era grocery, Silver City, housing a store from Cobalt's early days.

BOB CARLIN

Bob Carlin shortly before his death. Behind him is a photo
of the 1912 strike, and on the right, Big Jim McGuire.

ROYAL FLUSH

Royal visitor: The Prince of Wales in 1919, with the boarded-up
Jamieson Meat Market in the background.

SNOW STEPS

Winter on Grandview Avenue with miners Jim Jones and Mike Ruddy.

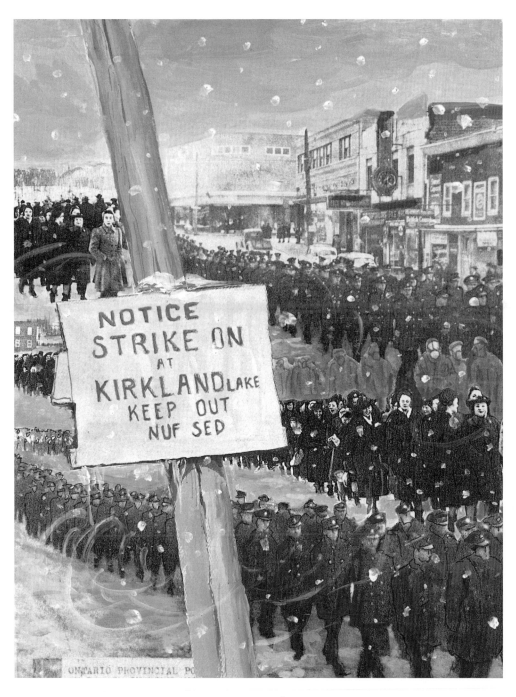

STRIKE!

Scenes from the 1941 Kirkland Lake Mine strike: The march of Hepburn's
Hussars (500 OPP) through Kirkland Lake, followed by the two-mile
walk of wives and children in defiance and support.

GRAVEYARD SHIFT

Miners going underground at Agnico Silver Mine in 1943, watched over
by John Matson and Henry Chortier of the Silver Miller Mine.

LAUNDRY DAY

Life below and above. The foreground shows a Mining Corporation crew in 1920;
above is the rescue team that saved a trapped miner at the O'Brien mine in 1954.

TOUGH TOWN

Bill Neal, rising to the challenge to pull a Volkswagen
from Haileybury to downtown Cobalt in 1970.

COBALT SATURDAY NIGHT

A scene from WeeBee's Bar with members of Cobalt's hockey team, the Silver Kings.
Freeman Smith (top right, with beard) makes an appearance.

RESTORATION

The Orpheum Theatre of yesterday unfolds to reveal
the restored Classic Theatre of today.

Gabriel Blows His Horn

I remember when they drilled into the centre of Cobalt Lake. They drilled underneath for months and put in all kinds of bulkheads with timber and had all the pumps ready at the station. They were trying to break through a big high-grade vein and when they pulled the switch, boom! Down she went. The blast went right through the bottom of the lake. The rush of the water and the slimes pushed everything back. Those bulkheads were just like match sticks. It flooded the mine and drained the lake. It's a crazy old town, but you can't tell people about these things because they'd never believe you.

– Joe Malick, retired miner, 1993

JOE MALICK was just a youth when he went to work in the mines of Cobalt. You had to be willing to work hard and long. Those who couldn't keep pace were sent packing. "They used to bring the rock from underground and dump it in the yard. Then they'd load it in trucks and take it to the mill. Do you know how they'd load it? Using six or seven men with shovels. My hands were all cracked wide open because the muck was so dry. At the end of the first week I had to put the shovel on my wrist because I couldn't hold the shovel anymore. But I hardened up. We shoveled eight big trucks every day, somedays nine. It made men out of us."

Oldtimers laugh when they tell today about how they could burn lighted cigarettes on their hands and not feel it through the hard callouses. Those cigarettes could prove troublesome in more ways than one. For those with the habit, the mine tolerated no dallying on the job. "You never had time for smokes while you were working because the boss would be watching. As soon as one truck was full another came. If he saw you rolling a cigarette, the boss would say, 'You don't like working here? Down the road!' Jeez, it was hard work."

The low demand for silver made for tough times in Cobalt. In 1935 the streetcar tracks that had made the Tri-Towns a model of public transit were torn up. There were not enough workers to ride the cars. Only twenty-five years before, James Fitzpatrick, first president of the Nipissing Central Railway, predicted that the trolleys would run until "Gabriel blew his horn." The same year the big mill on Nipissing Hill, which had long been a presence in the local landscape, burnt to the ground. No companies were interested in rebuilding it. Although Arthur Brocklebank managed to mine $68,590 out of the old Coniagas Mine in 1933, other operations were more modest. The caretaker at the once-mighty McKinley-Darragh Mine, searching through the old property, managed to glean a mere $1,200 from the depleted veins.

The Yorkshire Mining Company tried to make a go of a mine in Cobalt working with a small crew. On August 24, 1933, a fire broke out underground. Adelard Leonard and J. Kennedy were working underground at the time. Leonard managed to climb the ladder and suffered extensive burns escaping through the burning shaft house. Kennedy was trapped underground. Fifty men fought frantically to get him out, but were unable to get through the smoke. By the time a mine-rescue squad arrived from Kirkland Lake, the only task at hand was the retrieval of the body. In its annual report the Yorkshire Mine had to admit that it didn't hoist any silver or cobalt in the area that year. Operations were suspended.

One of the well-known mining promoters in Cobalt in the 1930s and '40s was A.B. Pilliner, a black man who operated the Nerlip Mine near Cross Lake. Locals remember Pilliner as a man who always had a big Cadillac and a blonde woman on his arm. Carlo Chitaroni worked at the Nerlip operation and says the mine was kept going because Pilliner knew how to hustle investors.

I worked for Mr. Pilliner for awhile over at Silver Cliff. He ran that mine all through the depression. If that was today he'd never have gotten that mine up and running. He had no money. He'd start with maybe a $100,000 and if they hit no ore, he'd close the mine down, leaving just a hoistman and a pump man to look after the place. Then he'd go down to the States and raise some more money. He'd come back and pay everyone who hadn't been paid in six months. Then we'd start all over again.

Toward the end of the 1930s, the dormant mining industry started to pick up because a new market for the reserves of cobalt had been discovered—Nazi Germany. Gerald Presse remembers that his father, Captain Presse, was working at the Agnico Property in North Cobalt, when shipments of cobalt were being sent to Germany every three weeks. "Germany was the only country in the world," he explains, "that had developed cobalt as an alloy for hardening steel. They were producing much ammunition and using the cobalt in hardening parts for the rifles."

For young men who were able to find work, the town still maintained numerous bootleg joints where men could spend their pay on drink. "Every second house was a blind pig," recalls Joe Malick, "and drinks were thirty-five cents. The best one was the one behind the church. You could fall out of the church right into the blind pig. You'd see the people come out of the French church on Sunday. All the wives would start talking together and then Jimmy and I and you, we'd get together and the first thing you know, we'd all slip off and then head to the bootleggers."

The bootleggers faced the occasional raid from zealous police. One bootlegger hired two cabinetmakers to build casings wide enough to hold bottles. When the police came, the bottles were conveniently hidden in the walls. Other police were known to frequent the bootleggers themselves. Although the bootleggers served an exclusively male clientele, they were often run by women. Many were from families of Italian or East European backgrounds. When the mine money moved up to Kirkland Lake, many well-known bootleggers followed and reestablished their business up there.

The depression coincided with unparalleled growth in the gold camps further north. Canada was the second largest producer of gold in the world, and 75 percent of it was coming from the rich deposits in Kirkland Lake and the Porcupine. While communities around the world were withering, these towns blossomed.

In 1930 the mines of Kirkland Lake paid out $6 million in dividends. Four years later they paid out $20 million. In 1934 President Roosevelt increased the price of gold from $20 an ounce (US) to $35. This massive increase caused a fury of activity in the gold regions. Within three years, the workforce directly employed by Kirkland Lake mines rose from three thousand to eight thousand men.

In Timmins, the big producers like Hollinger and McIntyre (Hollinger Mines was employing twenty-nine hundred men in 1937) were in continual expansion, while a whole series of new mines were opening. Rich mines like the Broulan Reef, the Delnite, and the Preston all began operations. Armand Coté left Cobalt in the late 1930s to work at the newly opened Pamour Mine on the edge of South Porcupine. Timmins saw its population rise from thirteen thousand at the beginning of the decade to twenty-five thousand by the end of it.

Other miners found that work was available across the border in Rouyn-Noranda and down through the fabled Valley of Gold that was beginning to open up in Quebec. Cobalters made themselves at home in the towns of Malartic and Val d'Or. But the trained miners in Cobalt had to compete in all these towns with hordes of men who had come from across the country, lured by the hope of getting work in the gold mines. They descended on these towns creating desperate line-ups every day outside the mine gates.

To be selected for work was like winning the lottery. Men who came from factories in the south or off the farm were inexperienced and at a considerable disadvantage

compared to the Cobalt boys. One oldtimer remembers the shift boss suspiciously ask-
ing a man if he had any experience in mining. "Sure," the man lied, "I worked in the
Kirkland Lake Gold Mine." "Well," said the shift boss, testing him, "what kind of
lights do they use there?" "I dunno," the fellow replied, "I was always on the day shift."

Dan Hellens was a Cobalt boy who managed to find work in the Wright-Hargreaves Mine at a time when the manager had a policy of firing the man on each shift
whom he thought worked the slowest. Cuthie Dixon and Pap Hylands left Cobalt for
work in Kirkland Lake. They were hired not because of their experience but because
they proved that they were skilled hockey players. Other men were hired if they had a
talent on the saxophone or violin. Kirkland Lake maintained a top-quality touring
band, and good musicians could always find work in the accounting or assaying offices
of the local mines.

Of all the gold towns, Kirkland Lake was the most notorious. It was run like a feudal enclave under the control of men like Sir Harry Oakes, owner of the Lakeshore
Mine, and Bill Wright, the owner of the Wright-Hargreaves Mine. Wright owned the
Toronto *Globe* and shamelessly used it as a soapbox against unions, higher taxes, and
regulations on his golden goose in Kirkland Lake.

One hundred men were killed in the mines of Kirkland Lake between 1929 and
1939. And an even greater toll was being exacted from the silica-laden rock that surrounded the gold ore. Myrtle MacLeod moved with her husband, Sam, from Cobalt
in 1929. Sam was twenty-four years old and in peak physical condition when he left the
defunct Cobalt operations. Because of his youth, good health, and his experience in
the mines in Cobalt, he was hired on at the Lakeshore Mine.

The work was hard and relentless. Sam worked seven days a week and on Sundays
he did a double shift, ending one at three in the afternoon and returning for the
evening shift at seven. In October of 1929, Sam was working in a raise when he was
overcome by poisonous gas. Fellow workers managed to pull him out; he was given a
shot of oxygen and sent home. "I'll never forget how I felt," says Myrtle MacLeod, now
in her eighties, "when I saw him being brought home being held up by a man on each
arm, in the middle of a Sunday morning."

Although Sam was deemed able to return to work, his lungs had been irreparably
damaged. The silica dust continued to aggravate the tissue and by the time he was in
his early thirties, Sam was falling victim to the cancer that would eventually kill him.[*]

With an ever-present mob of men wanting work, a miner thought twice about
making any complaints about working conditions. Any man unwilling to risk working
in unsafe conditions knew that there were dozens of others who would. Any talk of
unionizing could leave them standing outside the gates with the mob.

---

[*]When he was forced to retire in 1968 at the age of 62 because his health was completely shattered, Sam
MacLeod was given a pension of $13.50 a year from the Lakeshore Mine.

Bob Carlin was a hoistman at the Teck Hughes mine in Kirkland Lake. He had worked hoist for thirteen years without missing a single day of work, but on February 1, 1940, he was one of forty-seven men fired from the mine for having signed union cards. Carlin, who had come of age during the bitter 1919 strike in Cobalt, knew that the companies were getting ready to fight a decisive battle with their workers. He became a main organizer in the drive to restore the union.

In 1941 the discontent that had been brewing in Kirkland Lake for some time blew up in a general strike of the area's mines. Coming at the height of the war, the strike was bitter and controversial. The Kirkland Lake strike became a landmark in Canadian labour history. Although it ended in apparent failure, it changed forever the prospects for union organizing in Canada. The government came to the realization that to win a war it needed the support of labour, and it passed the historic order-in-council PC 1003, which recognized the right of workers to organize and bargain collectively.

This recognition was little comfort to the miners of Kirkland Lake, who faced mass firings and retribution in the aftermath of the strike. In the upheaval following the strike, thousands of gold miners made the migration to Sudbury. The International Nickel Company (INCO) ruled Sudbury as its private domain. "There were always three shifts at INCO," locals used to joke, "one working, one being hired, and one being fired." But among the many gold miners who came to work in Sudbury during the war were union activists like Bob Carlin. They stunned the company and industry in general when, in 1944, they succeeded in certifying the union throughout INCO's Sudbury properties. For the first time since the days of Jim McGuire, the miners were standing on solid ground.

CHAPTER FIFTEEN

The War Years

We were listening to the radio when we heard the Prime Minister declare war on Germany. My brother said, "that's it for me." He quit the mine and left right away to join up. Soon after, all the other men left to join the army.

– a local woman

When I think of the war, I can't help but think of the women. How in hell did the women come through the depression when their children were hungry and needing clothing, when the government told them there was no money to help? Then the war came and suddenly costs meant nothing to the government. They picked them up by the carload and dressed them in the best shoes and fixed up their teeth. They took all these boys from their mothers and now they are dead. George Cherniak was one of them. He was a Ukrainian lad from the end of Short Lake. While we were out sleighriding, he was at home studying. His mother used to have to come along and blow out the lamp. We lost that young man. We lost so many fine young men. It's unbelievable how these women came through all this and were able to stand it.

– John Gore

ONE OF THE FINEST collections of war memorabilia in the country is housed in the former train station in Cobalt. Created by World War II veteran Jimmy Jones, the Bunker Military Museum has become a major tourist attraction since it opened in the early 1990s. A war museum in Cobalt? In many ways it makes perfect sense. Memories of the war remain very prevalent. Every Remembrance Day, the town is shut down while a large group of veterans, schoolchildren, and locals pay their respects to the dead. As the flag is lowered, the names of local men who died during both wars is read out. The list amounts to almost one hundred names—quite a toll in a town too small to have streetlights. After the names are read out, the wreaths are laid. Some are from local businesses, many are from families who still mourn. More than half a century has passed, but the tears still flow in Cobalt on November 11.

When Canada declared war on a warm September evening in 1939, the Algonquin Regiment (based out of the Tri-Towns) was 250 men strong, made up mostly of reservists and non-commissioned officers. It was a volunteer regiment, a spiritual descendant of the regiment that had left Cobalt under Captain Armstrong in World War I. On September 4, 1940, their ranks swelled with lumber workers, clerks, and miners, the Algonquin Regiment boarded the train bound for Camp Borden.

Local high-school principal and volunteer soldier, George Cassidy, documented the role played by the regiment in his book *Warpath: The Story of the Algonquin Regiment 1939-1945*. The Algonquins had their first experience of real war during the allied breakout from the Normandy bridgehead in the summer of 1944. In the Battle for the Falaise Gap, they forged a bloody road through battle-hardened German troops. The Algonquins remained in the thick of the fighting throughout the push into Belgium, through the hard fighting into Holland, and in the crossing of the Rhine. Many boys from the Tri-Towns and northern Ontario are buried in the fields of France and Holland.

The men who volunteered for the navy or air force went into action much earlier. Ralph Benner joined the air force at the outbreak of the war. "I joined up and waited six months for a call. It came three days before Christmas, 1940. I landed in England at Christmas, 1941. I was trained as a navigator and came out as a flight lieutenant. I was with the 429 Bison squadron and bombed on night duty."

Victor Miettenen was a handsome young Finnish boy who left the mines of the area to try his hand with the air force. Within three minutes of his first air mission for Coastal Command, he sighted and attacked a German submarine. Like many Canadians, he fell in love over in England and was married in 1944. Somewhere near Woking, England, a simple white cross reads:

Pilot Officer
V.V. Miettnen
Royal Canadian Air Force
31.7.44.
Victor was twenty-eight years old.

Many of the men who joined the navy were posted to the large fleet of corvettes, small ships assigned to protect the steady convoys of merchant shipping that left regularly from Halifax and Sydney. It was common for the corvettes to be given the name of a Canadian town and many a merchant ship looked out starboard to see the HMCS

Cobalt searching the brine for German submarines. Men onboard the HMCS *Cobalt* had the logo of a bee wearing a miner's helmet, wielding a miner's pick and waving a stick of dynamite at the German swastika.

The first serious invasion of Europe by the Allies was launched against the island of Sicily in 1943. Edith Fowke, the famous Canadian folk historian, mentions in her book *Folk Songs of Canada* that Canadian troops fighting in Sicily were met by peasants singing "The Cobalt Song." Perhaps this song was the only thing the peasants knew about Canada and they were trying to win favour with the advancing Canadians. No doubt the soldiers from the prairies and from cities like Montreal would have wondered what all this talk about hob-nail boots and gin rickies was about, especially when delivered in thick Sicilian accents!*

For a young child the war seemed like an eternity. Many of the men they longed for were in fact strangers to them. They had left so long ago and some of them would never be coming back. When the trains full of German prisoners would pull through Cobalt en route to the prisoner of war camp in Montieth, Ontario, children would stand along the tracks and wave. It was always a big thrill when the prisoners waved back. Perhaps this was the closest they could come to their own relatives overseas.

"My father," says Joan Montieth, "was among the first troops to go overseas. I was only three years old at the time. He was gone from August of 1940 until the end of 1945. Five years is a long time to be away. The way the war was, you never really knew where the men were or what they were involved in. The men were never allowed to tell you what was going on. Anytime they did send you information, it was blacked out."

Children growing up at this time took the extraordinary circumstances of wartime as normal. It was normal that there were no men in town, ordinary that there was rationing and ordinary that their little town of Cobalt was somehow tied up in a war that involved the whole world. They were connected to this world by the radio.

"I remember listening to the radio," recalls Vivian Hylands. "That was my world. I knew *Terry and the Pirates* backwards and forwards. I'd just rush home from school to listen to the radio programs. Most of the radio was concerned then with the war."

What did women do during war? According to Joan Montieth, "They stayed home. Well, you got your cheque at the end of the month and you went to the grocery store and paid your bill. Oh, maybe once a month you went to the Minerva Restaurant when the cheque came in and had ice cream. And when you went to the store you got a bag of cookies, store-bought cookies. That was it. Of course everything was rationed. And as a kid, you froze until Christmas because that's when you got your winter clothes, your boots."

---

*Fowke uses this anecdote to underline her point that "The Cobalt Song" endured long after the collapse of the silver boom and was the most famous Canadian mining song.

Canada was transformed by the war from a mostly agricultural and economically poor country into a major world power. This country of a mere eleven million mustered the third largest merchant fleet in the world, and a powerful air force. Its factories were supplying equipment not only for its own soldiers but for Russian and British soldiers as well. Canadian wheat and commodities were helping to keep Great Britain alive.

All of this was possible because of the great efforts made by ordinary citizens in towns across the country. It wasn't just that people were willing to ration and save materials needed in war production, they also became active producers of vital food and clothing products. The family economy became a war economy.

Vivian Hylands remembers the effort that went into local food production.

Everybody had a Victory garden. People put up their own jams and jellies. There were no freezers. We had to put the food up because there was no one here to feed us otherwise. The food was put in boxes, then they would take flour sacks and needles with string and it all had to be wrapped a certain way. We would never have won the war if we hadn't been able to feed ourselves and the servicemen overseas.

The war at home was waged by women, old people, and children. The work gave children like Vivian a tactile sense of the great war going on overseas.

Then of course there was the knitting. A tremendous amount of knitting was done for the war effort. We had piles of knitting books and knitted all the strange garments needed for the war: balaclavas, different kinds of things that went under the steel helmets, gloves with one or two fingers out for gunners, socks, everything. There was knitting for the air force, the navy, and the infantry. You didn't have to be a boy to know how they fought the war.

In a town that had few phones, the telegram represented the arrival of important news in the town. During the war, this kind of news was always bad. Joan Montieth remembers the sight of the Telegram Man.

The most horrendous person in town to see was the Telegram Man. When you saw him go to someone's house, you knew it was because it meant someone had died. There was no car and so everything was done by foot, and so you watched him come down the street, hoping he wasn't coming to your house.

Ernie Tressider remembers that after the telegram man left the house of an unfortunate family, a black ribbon was placed over the door so that people would know that tragedy had struck.

Early in May of 1945, allied troops met the advancing Russians in the ruins of Berlin. Suddenly it was all over. Vivian Hylands was on the train with her mother, returning from the west coast, when news of the German surrender was first heard. "I remember how my Uncle Don Russell had put champagne away for that day and how we got together to celebrate. It was terribly exciting but also exhausting, having just come off that long train ride."

Ernie Tressider remembers people rushing down to Cobalt Square after hearing the announcement on the radio. Finally, the nightmare was over and the town exploded in a spontaneous celebration of all the joy and thanksgiving that had been suppressed for six long years.

Then began the seemingly endless wait for loved ones and relatives to be returned home. The Alqonquins returned to Canada at the beginning of 1946, and arrived at the train station in North Bay on January 29. There was a raging snowstorm waiting to greet them at the station, but it didn't matter; the snow couldn't begin to dampen the excitement of the crowd waiting on the platform.

The relief of having the men come home was sometimes mixed with the uncertainty of greeting strangers. Some children had never known their fathers. Some women found the men who came home to them were very different from the ones to whom they had bid tearful farewells.

One Cobalt woman remembers the reunion. "The war took an awful toll on this town. Some men came back shellshocked; some had mental problems. I know my father was well on his way to alcoholism after he came back and it was the war that did it. Things were much harder after the war because of the alcohol. It was scary for some of the wives and children because these men came back as strangers."

Some of the young soldiers returned with women they had married overseas. Ralph Benner was one of them. "I was so glad to be back after the war. I still remember singing 'Oh Canada' when we came home. I was crying I was so glad to be back. Coming back to Canada—seeing lights on in homes and stores after three-and-a-half years of darkness. I found the houses very warm here. It took me a year or two to get used to central heating again."

They were coming home to a different Cobalt. "I remember coming home on the train," says Ralph Benner, " and I met Cal Taylor who was the MP for Temiskaming at that time. He told me that big things were happening in Cobalt." The long-awaited return of the boom was taking place. Much of the drive and energy for this new bonanza would come from the returning veterans like Ralph Benner.

CHAPTER SIXTEEN

The Days of
the Silver Miller

In 1919 Cobalt's vigour began to wane, the drills grew silent as the silver lode was lost. People began to move away, the town became what some called a ghost town. This name was very much resented by us oldtimers who believed in its revival. And this belief has been justified as we now have a brand new town, mostly because Harry Miller had the faith that would not be destroyed. We have today, in 1955, a beautiful mine set up in white and red on the very site of the original LaRose Mine.

– Elizabeth MacEwan, 1955

W HEN REG DOAN first went to work underground at the Brady Lake silver mine he was young and inexperienced. He didn't realize that the rich sheets of pure silver he bagged on his shift represented a geological and financial marvel. "After blasting we would return to find slabs of silver about a quarter of an inch thick curled up along the wall. We'd go over and take them and bend them up and down with our hands to break them off and put them in bags to take to surface. It was pure silver. When you drilled into the silver, the shavings would curl down like drilling into a block of wood. They were shavings of pure silver."

Shavings of pure silver. It had a ring that hadn't been heard in Cobalt since the early days of Fred LaRose. As the 1950s dawned, those days seemed to be back. Harry Miller, a local promoter, had started the ball rolling when he hit high-grade silver in an old mining property on Brady Lake. Miller's company, Silver Miller Mines, was one of several small operations that began development work in Cobalt as the war was winding down. The Brady Lake operation propelled Harry Miller into the forefront of the mining resurgence in the Cobalt camp. By the early 1950s, Miller was operating three very profitable operations—Brady Lake, the Lawson, and the reborn LaRose Mine.

The reopening of the LaRose property was perhaps the most visible symbol of the town's rebirth. Right in the centre of town, the main shaft was being refitted and a new concentrator built. For young men there was work to be had. M. J. Scully spent his summers working in these reopened mines while studying at the seminary in the fall.

"I used to walk to mass at Ste.Thérèse at seven o'clock. I'd pack an extra lunch, get half way up the hill, sit down, and have a few sandwiches, then carry on to work. At that time they still hadn't rebuilt the LaRose shaft so we used to have to go underground by climbing in the big open cuts that are on the property. I guess you might say that was the last summer I spent working for a living."

The success of Harry Miller was a great impetus to many other mining promoters. What really aided the boom of the 1950s, however, was the sudden interest in the base metal cobalt. During the first silver rush, cobalt was often looked upon as more of a hindrance than a blessing. Prospectors looking for the quick riches of high-grade silver tossed this enigmatic base metal out on the dump piles.

But demand for the goblin metal had risen dramatically. The cold war was in full swing and the American government was pushing to build its reserves of strategic metals. The mineral cobalt was used in the hardening of steel. The town of Cobalt had waited many years for the return of the Prince, and they found it in the value given to the "Cinderella mineral" (as local promoters began calling it). But this was a Dark Prince, born on the clouds of fear and war. Company reports from the silver camp boasted pictures of battleships, atomic explosions, and ballistic missiles. Such was the glamour of this deadly new world.

The search for cobalt was carried on in the same shafts that had once been used for silver exploration. The LaRose Mine hoisted almost fifty thousand tons of cobalt ore in 1955. The Right of Way, the Crown Reserve, Kerr Lake, the O'Brien, and Nipissing properties all made a comeback as shafts and drifts were dewatered and the crews went in to diamond drill the rock. Diamond drilling revealed deposits that had been overlooked.

Carlo Chitaroni, mine captain at the Lawson Mine, recalls that the discovery of new deposits in old properties was sometimes simply a matter of running water over the faces of old stopes. Since many of the early operations did not use water on their drills, the stopes would be covered with dust after blasting. Some mines ran out of money before checking behind the thick mounds of dust thrown up by the last blast.

Even though mining elsewhere had become increasingly scientific, in Cobalt it still remained a matter of playing the odds. The erratic nature of the geology defied planning. Cobalt didn't offer ore bodies, instead it was like looking for buried treasure—rich pockets of ore trapped in barren host rock. Consequently, it was a more fitting climate for young companies: they took risks on properties that bigger companies would pass over. These reborn operations were like lotteries. An old property might yield a rich new discovery, but there was no guarantee. Many companies had runs of luck lasting a year or two, only to grind to a humiliating halt when the silver veins suddenly ran dry.

Ralph Benner returned from the war to finish his geology degree and then made his way back to Cobalt. He teamed up with fellow war veterans Hal Kenty and Dan Hellens, as well as Mario D. Bastianni. They decided to try their luck on a property just down from the Silver Miller operation at Brady Lake.

"We were all close friends. Dan and I became partners. With Mario's help and guidance we pumped the shaft and fixed it all up for operation. The first drill we put down struck high-grade silver. It was the first money I made and to celebrate Dan, Mario, and I went to Purdy's Lunch Counter and had a round of cokes."

The mine they developed, the Cobalt Lode, was a good producer in the early years of the 1950s.

In the big mining camps the technology of underground production had made great advances, but mining hadn't really changed in Cobalt. While miners at the Frood mine in Sudbury were hauling ore underground with electric ore trains, miners in Cobalt continued pushing the old, one-ton cars by hand to be hauled to surface. The gold mines in Kirkland Lake had reached below eight thousand feet in depth, but most mines in Cobalt remained at about five hundred feet. Mike Farrell remembers how the ground shook underground at the LaRose Mine when the Ontario Northland train went overhead. The LaRose Mine was so shallow that miners on the evening shift sometimes climbed up the vent raise and scurried over to the Miners' Home Tavern.

Carlo Chitaroni says that the high-grade ore in the Cobalt camp was still being hand "cobbed" underground and put into bags. The local mills simply couldn't extract all the wealth of the ore and too much could be lost in the waste dumps.

If the silver or cobalt vein was really pure the mines picked and slashed it, then put it in bags. They always slashed the ore and cobbed it because if you send it to the mill, you're going to lose some. Sometimes if you had a vein that was really rich you might lose half of it if you sent it to the mill.

In the bigger mines, the job of mucking out ore had been mechanized for some time. In some of the big base metal mines, the companies were beginning to experiment with rubber-tired diesel loaders (scoop trams) which could dwarf the work of even the mucking machine. But time stood still in Cobalt. Mucking was still the domain of the shovel and a strong back. Mike Farrell recollects:

The big mines in Sudbury, Timmins, and Kirkland Lake were all using mucking machines. But in Cobalt we were still using shovels to muck the ore. There was only one mucking machine at the LaRose. The rest of it was done by hand. When

*I think about how we broke our backs then to make a buck, mucking and tram-
ming twenty-five or thirty one-ton cars out of the back stope and into the cage to
send them up, and today one diesel scoop tram could come along in one scoop or
two scoops and do what it took old Mike Farrell all day to do by hand.*

Even though the work was harder, Mike Farrell remembers that there was more give
and take in the smaller operations of Cobalt.

*I worked in an open cut just below the big original open cuts that had been
worked in the first boom. We were working down about thirty feet and had to be
extremely careful because we were working over an open stope that had been
mined at the old LaRose. We had to put in timbers to make our way across. Bill
Dunn was my partner. Come blasting day we'd finish off work around lunch
time. We'd load the holes with powder and then we'd climb out of the cuts in our
gear and head down to the bank at lunch time. You could never leave in your
muckers and gear at the big gold mines. Then we'd run across to the Legion for a
few quick drinks. Then we'd hit the liquor store and head back up to the mine. It
might be one of those really hot days and we'd sit in that open cut feeling the
beautiful cool air coming up from underground, and drink all afternoon. Pep
Chitaroni, who was our shift boss, used to shake his head saying, "I don't know
how you guys could show up for work sober and go home drunk." You know, we
never made much money then, but we sure had a lot of fun.*

Young miners might have found ways to have fun on the job, but it still remained very
much a front-line experience. In the five years that Reg Doan worked at Silver Miller,
he remembers the men killed in the local mining community.

*Mr. Brunette was pinned to the wall by a loaded car of ore. He was alive and talk-
ing to the rescuers until they removed the car. He had been so badly crushed he
died almost instantly once the weight of the car was taken off his chest. Felice
Maloney fell down a raise at Brady Lake. He broke his back and died. Percy Valley was crushed when the hoist moved while he was unloading some timbers.
Rene Sauvé was killed at the Cobalt Lode and Wayne Parcher was killed a couple
of years after that. This is a very high statistic for the 250 or so men working in
town.*

A new push for better safety standards came to the fore again as the union renewed its
presence in town. The United Steelworkers sent Pat Burke into Cobalt in 1950 to organize the Cobalt Foundry and the Silver Miller Mine. Recalls Doan: "The union did
bring better pay and better working conditions. Prior to the union coming into the

foundry, you went home in the same clothes you wore to work. You couldn't wash at the foundry. After the union came in, they brought in showers and such. Things slowly improved. The mines were the same way."

John Gore remembers how difficult it was to maintain the profile of the union when membership remained voluntary. "I used to have to go into the beer halls to collect union dues off these guys. I was called pretty much everything but late for dinner." It wasn't until 1954 that the Silver Miller local managed to negotiate the first compulsory checkoff for a miners' local in northern Ontario. It was a big breakthrough, helped by the fact that the Silver Miller manager, Milt Halstead, was recognized as a man of progressive views.

But pressure soon came from the big companies in Kirkland Lake as well as from Noranda Mines (over in Rouyn-Noranda, Quebec) to force the small silver company to take a harder line with the workers. Labour activist Don Taylor, who got his first union experience with the Silver Miller local believes that companies like Noranda feared that if the Cobalt miners were successful it would lead to pressure at the bigger mines for fairer wages and union recognition. Within a year, many of the leadership of the local had been laid off or fired under a variety of pretexts.

Reg Doan became active in the local at this time. "When I think back it was one of the poorest times of my life. It was very hard to raise a family on the wages that were paid in the mines and I was making top wages then—$1.53 an hour." Over two negotiated contracts, Silver Miller refused to grant wage increases. When the contract ended in March 1956, the union demanded a raise of fifteen cents an hour. Silver Miller stated they couldn't afford it. The men asked to see the books. If the claim was true, they would accept a compromise. The company refused. Both company and miners knew they were on a collision course and the workplace grew increasingly tense. On August 5, 1956, the Silver Miller miners went out on a five-week wildcat strike. "We weren't in a legal position to strike until November," recalls Doan, "but that would have meant the men had to strike in winter and we knew the men couldn't hold up under the extreme winters we have in Cobalt."

The town had been pretty tense in the weeks leading up to the strike. People knew that the men were ready to go out at any time.

Once we set up the picket line, the men were very cooperative. We set up strike tents at the three properties; Brady Lake, the Lawson, and the LaRose Mine. We checked the cars to make sure that only company officials were going into the site. It was a complete shutdown, except that we agreed to allow the foremen and company management employees to keep pumps running so the mines wouldn't flood.

Because it was a wildcat strike, the Local was unable to receive support from the Steelworkers International. They got by on donations of canned goods and the goodwill of other locals. But goodwill was in short supply at the Silver Miller, as management took a hard line and refused to negotiate.

> *The mining companies in Kirkland Lake pressured the Silver Miller Mine not to negotiate with us. The Kirkland Lake gold mines sent a professional personnel man on loan. He did all of the talking at any meetings we attended. The local mine managers were almost not allowed to speak. He made all the decisions and adopted a hard line. It was clear they were out to win the strike.*

At the end of five weeks, the men received letters from the Labour Board informing them that they were involved in an illegal strike and could be fined up to $1,000 a day each if they didn't return to work. A vote was held to go back to the negotiating table and accept the best possible deal.

Reg Doan was one member of the six-man negotiating team. "We had made a promise at the beginning of the strike that we wouldn't go back for anything less than fifteen cents an hour. So we went to the meeting and five out of the six of us quit our jobs on the spot. There was me, Ernie Bilodeau, Leo Scully, Red Kingston, and Alf Dubé. That was pretty much it for us in Cobalt and we left to find work elsewhere." Red Doan said that for years after the strike he was blacklisted in the Tri-Towns area as an agitator.

As the decade wore on, the Silver Miller star began to wane. The rich high-grade pockets wore out, and new drilling failed to locate enough new deposits to keep the company going. There remained a host of small companies having erratic luck in the Cobalt camp, each of them struggling to claim the glory that had been held for a time by Harry Miller.

As Silver Miller Mines began laying off men, the sudden demand for experienced men in the boom camp of Elliot Lake led to a major exodus of young men. The discovery of uranium on the "big Z" north of Blind River had led to a chaotic wild boom unseen since the early days of Cobalt. The American government, in its desire to stockpile uranium, offered to buy whatever could be mined. This sudden demand for uranium drew some of the best men in the industry to the bush camp forming at Elliot Lake. Ralph Benner and many of his compatriots joined the search—making history with the opening of Denison Mine in Elliot Lake.

Where other rushes had been accomplished with wagon trains and the railway, this rush was one of Buicks and Fords. The ride into Elliot Lake took as long as thirteen hours due to the makeshift roads. Cars that broke down were left by the side of the road to be stripped by parts-hungry seekers. The men were housed in tents, and in the rush to fulfill the uranium orders, men who had never held a drill before were sent underground—sometimes still in their street clothes. It was a chaotic trek that brought almost thirty thousand people in three years to Elliot Lake.

Many Cobalters were part of this trek. Georgie Church recalls how her husband left to find work in the uranium mines. "My husband Buddy and his friends heard about jobs in Elliot Lake. They had only two dollars in their pocket and they hitch-hiked out there. Once they were gone, the wives were left in Cobalt not knowing if they got a job or whether they were even alive. You just didn't hear from them. People didn't phone back and forth like they do now."

Reg Doan and his blacklisted partner Ernie Bilodeau headed to the Milliken Mine in Elliot Lake. He was shocked by the conditions underground. "The air was thick with a terrible, blue smoke." While many Cobalt men stayed, Reg decided there was something terribly wrong in the mines of Elliot Lake and moved on.

The wild boom didn't last. In 1959, the American government cancelled their contract. Ten mines closed almost overnight and the great boomtown of Elliot Lake became almost a ghost town. Many things had changed since the early days in Cobalt, but the wild rise and brutal bust of a mineral rush wasn't one of them.

CHAPTER SEVENTEEN

Hanging Out at the Minerva

So many things have changed since I was younger. I guess television has changed our life. I know the automobile certainly has.

– Ernie Tressider, retired store owner, 1994

V IVIAN HYLANDS lives in the old mill manager's house on what was once the Buffalo Mine. Her uncle owned this house at one time, and before that, it was owned by the manager of the Buffalo mill. One night in early winter she invited us over to her house, which locals refer to as the Buffalo House. She wanted to reminisce about being a teenager during Cobalt's second boom. From her hangout near the jukebox and soda machine, she watched the excitement of a town being reborn.

Things were very prosperous in the 1950s. We had stores like TBS (Toronto Bargain Store) and Buckovesky's. Mr. Herbert still had his store and Mr. Staedleman had his music store. Frank Costello was running Moore's Drug Store and Mr. Shaw was running his drug store. There was the Minerva and the Boston, George's Pool Room, and the Panarites' Candy Store. When the older people—the mine managers and the business people—went uptown, they went to the Boston Grill. We teenagers, on the other hand, hung out at the Minerva. It was very American, just what you'd think a fifties restaurant was like. It had booths and stools. We used to go there after school or after the show to have an ice-cream soda.

Vivian's sister Judy made the leap from the juvenile gatherings at the Minerva to the Boston Grill when she returned from Shaw's Business School in Toronto. Judy became a secretary for a well-known Queen's Counsel in Haileybury, Dalton Dean, who had made his reputation working on the Nuremberg War Crimes Tribunal. As a staff member of a well-respected law firm, Judy was expected to make her social calls at the Boston. For a young person, that took nerve.

Charlie Ferris, the son of Syrian parents who had come to Cobalt in the early days, ran the Boston Grill. He was well known for his rich selection of candy, much of it homemade. Young people were welcome to come in and buy the candy, but they were not encouraged to make themselves at home. Joan Montieth remembers stocking up on the Boston Grill's penny candy before heading off to the picture show. "As soon as you walked in, they glared at you and said, 'Keep your hands off the candy.'"

When Helene (Scully) Culhane started going into the store in the early 1970s, very little had changed.

There was candy everywhere. Candy, candy, candy, and Charlie Ferris made most of it himself. His mother hardly spoke any English. She was Syrian. If you pointed to a candy you wanted, she'd slap your hand and say, "Don't touch the candy." It took all your nerve to sit down on the stools and say, "Can I have a cherry coke, please?" He'd serve them in those little coke glasses. We'd watch him mix it up and stir it. Then he'd give it to us and stare at us until we finished it. We'd gulp it down and say thank you very much and get the hell out of there.

In 1954 Paul Oblin opened the Green Lantern Restaurant on Lang Street. It was the closest Cobalt would come to the bohemian fad of that period. Paul Oblin's neighbour was Tommy Black. Tommy Black ran a hardware store. He had first opened his store in 1913 and ran one of the oddest hardware businesses ever. Locals love to recount their attempts to buy merchandise in Tommy Black's store. Mr. Black often insisted they buy it where it was cheaper. If they gave him an argument, he might just chase them out. Paul Oblin remembers:

When I was renting the Green Lantern in 1954, I had smashed up all the sidewalk to put in a new sidewalk. I went into his store to buy a sledgehammer and he asked what I wanted it for. I told him and he said, "How long will you have it for, brother?" "A few days, Tom." So he went into the display case and said, "Now you make sure you don't damage this, and bring it back when you're done." He wouldn't sell it to me. Everything you'd buy, he'd criticize the price. If you tried to buy a coffee pot he'd say, "Do you know what I have to charge for this piece of junk? Do you know what they want me to make you pay?" If a lady came into the store and was a little bit bossy, he'd refuse to sell to her. "If you think I'm going to climb that ladder so you can look at those teacups, then lady, you're mistaken."

M. J. Scully remembers going into the store one time and seeing plates on the floor covered with a thick layer of dust. When he began to clean them off he realized that they were very fine china. "Don't clean it off," Black commanded. "If anyone knows fine china, they'll recognize it through the dust, and if they can't recognize fine china, I don't want to make it any easier for them." One time when Tommy was sick, he left his son in charge of the store. When people asked the son how Tommy was feeling, the son replied very matter of factly, "My father told me to tell anyone who inquired that it was none of their goddamn business."

How Mr. Black managed to stay in business for so many years (1913 to 1960) was always a matter of popular conjecture. He was a shrewd player of the stock market, according to some. Others speculated that the crates of fine china contained bootlegged alcohol. Most just believed that Tommy Black stayed in business because he belonged there, a figure of interest on the odd landscape that is Cobalt.

In the 1950s you could still find anything from fine suits to ice cream. It is a far cry from today, when there are five places where you can buy liquor in town, but no place to buy a bag of nails or a pound of meat. Yet there are those who would suggest that the signs of deterioration in Cobalt's business community were already appearing in the years following the war.

Before the war, Cobalt was the major business centre in the area. Cars weren't common. Many families didn't have refrigeration facilities at home. Shopping was done locally with grocery stores in every neighbourhood. Making the fifteen-minute drive up to New Liskeard would have been a big outing for most families and it was far more common to do one's shopping in the neighbourhood. "When my brother Ivan and I opened up our grocery store back in the '50s," recalls Ernie Tressider, "there were eleven grocery stores in Cobalt and thirty-five grocery stores throughout the Tri-Towns. And the population wasn't that much different than it is today. Now only three or four exist in the whole area."

This change in perspective was greatly accelerated at the war's end. For the first time, consumer patterns were beginning to determine social life. In bigger centres, the automobile and the rising individualism of the post-war generation was altering old notions of neighbourhood and community. Young families moved in droves to new housing developments in the suburbs.

John Gore still finds himself struck by the casualness with which modern culture has taken to commuting distances.

"We lived in a completely different world back then. My own son and grandson just went up to Fairbanks, Alaska, to race in the big dog races. When I was young, going to Fairbanks was like going to the moon. But they think nothing of driving that distance. I don't like driving to New Liskeard in March, let alone Alaska!"

New Liskeard, a fifteen-minute drive from Cobalt, was a perfect town for the 1950s. Surrounded by wide open plains, it could build bigger stores, provide more parking, and offer the latest services. Cobalt, on the other hand, was a town defined by its geography and its history. The twisting streets offered poor parking opportunities. In a town built around rock dumps and crevices, there was little room for expansion. In the years to come, shops that could expand and accommodate larger numbers of cars would begin to take away the business of the shopkeepers who still did their business on the streets of a long-spent frontier town.

The 1950s saw the rise in urban centres of the now familiar consumer-based identity. But at the time, it was barely noticeable in the tightly knit neighbourhoods of Cobalt. Still, the door had been opened and there was no going back. "I remember the first refrigerator I saw," recalls Joan Montieth. "It was like, wow. An electric refrigerator! Being poor wasn't so hard before, because everybody was in the same position. Everybody heated their houses with coal stoves. It didn't matter if you were well-to-do or not, that was just the way it was. But after the war the differences began to show."

The change was most noticeable in the aspirations of the younger generation. In the years before the war, working-class youth rarely made it to university or college. For years the only hope of advancement for many miners' sons lay in getting a trade or clerical position. In the 1950s this began to change. For the first time it was possible for a young person, if their parents had sweated, saved, and sacrificed, to go on to higher education.

"You have the problem," explains John R. Hunt, a journalist who first arrived in Cobalt in the early 1950s, "that the best and the brightest often leave. We had a very good high school, which seemed to take kids from very ordinary working-class families and motivate them so they could accomplish whatever they wanted to accomplish. Most of the best and the brightest have, by and large, got out."

Joan Montieth was sixteen when she decided to leave Cobalt. She had no real opportunities for school, but she felt she could fare better down south than in Cobalt.

> What was so unappealing about being a miner's wife? My father was a miner, and I knew what it was like. If there was work, there was work. If there wasn't, what were you going to do in the meantime? I remember my mother saying she'd rather starve than go on welfare. I didn't want to become a miner's wife and have children at seventeen. What else were you going to do? Work in a restaurant? In those days, the fifties, a girl was a second-class citizen. You didn't get the job if a man could take it.

For people who chose to leave for the greater opportunities offered in the south, there was a trade-off. While they were able to make more individualistic lifestyle choices, they often missed the strong sense of community. Joan Montieth found herself coming home every summer. While her children were growing up, she tried to make sure that they could spend as much of their summers as possible in Cobalt. But after many years in the city, she realizes she could never be fully held by such bonds. "I could never live here now. The gossip is really bad in this town. My brother Eddie used to say that if you walked into the Fraser Hotel and everybody stopped talking, then you knew your wife was cheating on you."

And so, like many who made the migration to the industrial centres of the south, Joan Montieth sees Cobalt as a home to come back to for her "two months of sanity." People like Joan live in cities all across the country, and they continue to come home to the small towns that were too small for them to live in, but much too important to ever leave behind.

CHAPTER EIGHTEEN

Playing in the Drifts

When I was sent to the group home I put on boxing gloves and beat every kid in the home. I was only twelve and some of them were eighteen, but I was from Cobalt. We were as tough as steel in Cobalt.

– Freeman Smith, local country singer, 1993

IT WAS THE MOVIES. The world of dreams and fantasies far beyond the confines of a small, dusty mining town could be touched at the movies. This is the way it had been since the early days in Cobalt. Generations of children glimpsed a world of tinsel and glory at the old Classic Theatre in Cobalt.

"When an Elvis picture would come to town," Freeman recalls, "we'd go along the road collecting pop bottles to get money to see the picture. Sometimes we'd walk all the way to Haileybury. We might collect two dollars worth of empties, but that, for a kid, was a fortune. Movies cost only thirty-five cents. Soon as the snow started to leave we'd get the cardboard boxes out and start walking. The empties would get heavy after a while, but we walked everywhere. I never owned a bike."

In the early 1960s the power of the movie house was being challenged for the first time. Across the continent, the television was altering notions of entertainment, culture, and even family. The living rooms of countless homes were being rearranged; instead of having sofas and chesterfields facing each other so people could talk, they were being set up around the centralizing presence of the television set.

In Cobalt, the power of the television was still limited by the lack of stations. Until the 1970s there were no options other than the CBC. Many parents tended to view this new member of the family with suspicion. They were from a generation that could not tolerate seeing children lying like vegetables on the living room floor for hours after school. Peter Larabie remembers how his access to the television was very restricted.

"We never went in the house. It's not like today. We never watched TV. We weren't allowed to. Well, we could watch *Ed Sullivan* or *Bonanza*, but that was about it. As soon as school was out, we'd be playing road hockey. They had to drag us in for supper and then it was back out again. When you live in a small house with six brothers and sisters you need the room, I guess."

It was a time before Nintendo and satellite TV began to bulldoze the cultural land-scape, when the power of children's entertainment lay in their own imaginations. Peter Larabie feels that this is perhaps the biggest change between his youth and that of the children he sees playing on the streets today.

"We didn't have the things kids have today, but we kept ourselves busy with so many things. We played baseball, archery, and guns; we played music. On Saturday mornings we'd grab a twenty-two rifle and leave. We'd go up to the hills with a frying pan and a potato in each pocket—with that you were good for the day. Kids today seem to need to be entertained. They can't entertain themselves."

Freeman Smith kept himself entertained as a boy, perhaps a little too entertained. "I was a bad little fella," he says casually. "Well, not really bad, but I had a bit of a disci-pline problem. You see, kids then didn't get the kind of breaks they do now." For a boy looking for trouble, Cobalt offered endless opportunities.

> We used to have a lot of fun playing in the mine shafts. We'd walk down through the shafts and where there was ice on the bottom we'd put our beer so it would stay cold. We'd get the winos off the corner to buy us beer or a couple of bottles of wine. At that time we would have been between nine and eleven years old. We'd get half lit in the shaft and then when we'd come up to the surface, the sun would hit us and we'd almost pass out. I think now how fortunate we were that none of us got alcohol poisoning because it was nothing for us to drink a couple of bottles of wine.

Under the streets of Cobalt, children discovered for themselves a nether world. Some made their way through the darkness with torches made from cloth wrapped around hockey sticks. Some played tag in the old drifts and others, hide and seek. They learned where to get access and followed the paths through the darkness, relying on old pipe lines and rusted rail track.

"When we were down in the shaft we used to go across the air lines, they'd be about ten or twelve inches in diameter. We'd walk out on those lines over a five-hundred-foot drop and then we'd hang like bats upside down. If your foot ever slipped you were history. I used to go with my cousin Bony Galliot and Ricky Heikilla. I remember when Ricky Heikilla tried to jump down the shaft on a dare. I just caught him in time."[*]

The air lines that once carried the compressed air from the Ragged Chutes Hydro plant provided ample opportunity for daredevils. Peter Larabie remembers running

---

[*] Rick Heikilla later died in an underground accident while working at a mine in British Columbia.

along the air pipes over open shafts. "About five years ago I went up to the spot where we used to run across the shafts. I couldn't even go near the edge. I was scared to get too close because of the drop. And to think we used to just run across it."

The danger was apparent but not appreciated. "One of my buddy's brothers fell down one of the shafts one time and they had to get the fire truck to go get him out," says Freeman Smith. "He fell a hundred feet and he got caught on a piece of wood and that was the only thing that saved him. The only one who ever got killed was Chuckie Graminski's brother. They were up playing at a shaft and the boards were rotted out. He ran across, fell through, and that was it."

Even on surface, children were able to transform an industrial wasteland into a playground. Some kids made pottery out of discarded tailings. Others remember collecting mercury off the ground in the late 1960s and bringing their collections to school. A popular game was called pancaking—children would jump up and down on the tailings ponds to see if their feet would get stuck in the quicksand-like slimes. One little girl, walking home from Cobalt Public School on a trail that ran over the old Coniagas tailings, became stuck in the slimes and drowned. Her school was built on top of an old mine shaft and the schoolyard abutted the slimes.

There were no serious fences to keep the children off these properties, no government ministry clean-ups demanded. Even today, there is a lingering ambivalence in many people about the need to secure the old sites and to fill in the open cuts. As adults they recognize the incredible dangers that old mine operations hold, yet there is a sense that something wild and untamed is being lost.

Since 1990, Ministry officials have been pressuring Agnico-Eagle Mines to clean up the old sites. The shafts have been capped, fences made secure, and some open cuts filled. But along with the clean-up have been plans that may include bulldozing the old mill foundations and "restoring" the original mine properties back to nature. The prospects of this reclamation have become a serious issue for the people of Cobalt. Many local people see the levelling of the old sites as a serious threat to the living memory of the community.

Perhaps the old ways of Cobalt can't survive in a world defined by notions of liability and public safety. Peter Larabie sums up the feelings of many people: "When we were young, if you could find a way into one of the new mines, it was something fantastic. Now all those properties are fenced in and there's warning signs up all over. I guess they had to do that, but you know, it kinda takes away from it all. It's really too bad."

For children who didn't play in the mine shafts, the town was still an endless source of adventure. Swimming at Bass Lake (four kilometres south of town) was a popular activity. Children would walk out along the highway or along the railway tracks to get there, and then spend the whole day playing and swimming in the cool waters. Lorie and Marta Church remember the ordeal of going to Bass Lake every day with their mother, Betsy, and Aunt Georgie.

Without a car of their own, the women would call a cab.

When the cab would pull up there'd be Georgie's kids (five of them), Joan Monti-eth's kids (two children), and the four of us. We'd all pile in. You could see the taxi driver getting nervous as more and more kids started to climb in. He would try to say, "Well, I gotta charge you extra." My mother would say, "What d'ya mean? Just drive!"

Helene Culhane remembers the defined horizons of life in a working-class town:

My father worked at the Wabi Iron Works in New Liskeard for thirty-two years and it killed him. He worked in terrible conditions. His breathing was awful and of course the smoking didn't help. He was a moulder and he hated his job. He was up every morning at five o'clock. He brought that paycheque home and handed it to my mother. How she stretched it with seven children, I'll never know. It still amazes me. We never had anything grandiose, but we never went without. We never went hungry. I had two older sisters and I was the hand-me-down queen.

Most children in her neighbourhood came from big families. Everything from getting ready for school to getting ready for bed was a major production.

We used to bath together. I would bath with my two older sisters, so there'd be Louise, Pat, and Helene in the tub. Then Louise hit puberty and she got out and Richard moved in. Louise got to bathe alone and then Pat, Helene, and Richard followed by Mark and Julie would bathe together. Pat hit puberty and in came Mark. That was the way you saved water. You couldn't get enough water to bathe us all at one time. Then there was the laundry for all of us. My mother did it with the ringer washer and it was always going in the kitchen. Everyone had wringer washers. There was the odd family that had more updated appliances, but you wouldn't know because you didn't really hang out with them.

Georgie Church was a young miner's wife raising five children and she remembers how people lived with a greater sense of community. "There were a lot of people not working. People lived really poorly. Nobody went away on holidays then or down to Toronto. It was a big thing to go down and watch the train come in. People were really good-hearted, more than they are now. Everyone seems to be for themselves now, and it sure wasn't like that then."

Georgie Church remembers the casual trust they had in the goodness of neigh-bours and even strangers. "One time this bill collector showed up at the house and he was giving me a hard time, and so I said, 'Just a minute, I'll go find my husband Buddy and get some money'. So I left and he was stuck babysitting my son Danny, who was just a baby. I went downtown to the Minerva. I met the gang, had a coke and some chips. I just left him there with the baby all day, and you know he never came back after that."

The world has changed a great deal since the early 1960s when people trusted the stranger. But has it changed that much in Cobalt? Like many small towns, people in Cobalt live with a great deal of trust in the goodwill of other people. The question often becomes one of whether today's generation has the same values and spirit that older generations had. When asked why her children complain of being bored and feel limited by a small town, Lorie Church says, "Well, all they want to do is play Nintendo. They don't want to get involved in anything more."

Marta Leopold isn't sure that the fault lies with the children. She sees it as something that has cut across the ages and is weakening the bonds of community involvement. "You can say the children don't want to get involved, but what about us? Englehart had a big play last week and none of us went. I don't know why that is. We used to go to all the plays. It's pretty bad when the high school puts on a play and nobody goes. It's not like we're out doing anything better."

CHAPTER NINETEEN

Fighting at the Fraser

The movies were always full. The rink was always busy. There used to be big all-night broom-ball tournaments. Teams would come from all the northern towns and there'd always be big fights upstairs at the arena. Hockey was really big. When we'd have games you'd have to get there really early to take tickets because it was always full. Everyone would go skating on Friday night. But it's all changed. People just stopped having carnivals and such.

– Georgie Church, nurse, 1993

T HE FRASER HOTEL dominates Cobalt's downtown. The three-story structure was once the toast of the north. In the days when it was the Royal Exchange Building, it boasted expensive suites and a mauve glass sidewalk lit from underneath. There is little of that glory left today. The upstairs rooms are little more than chipped plaster and broken light bulbs. The main floor, once a Stock Exchange, became a beer parlour in the 1930s.

The Fraser Hotel is a quiet place today. The bar is usually only patronized by a few regulars who huddle around the bar like the survivors of a great shipwreck. It could pass for any nicotine-stained beer parlour across the north. An old black-and-white photograph hanging on the wall above the pool tables provides the only clue as to what sort of town Cobalt was and what kind of people once drank at the Fraser. It is a photograph of the late Bill Neal dragging a car up Lang Street in front of a crowd of excited onlookers. The year was 1970 and Bill Neal, champion hand steeler and hand mucker, accepted the challenge to pull a Volkswagen from Haileybury to Cobalt (a five-mile trip). At the time, he was in his mid-fifties, but looked much older. What was the point of dragging the car? Simply because someone said it couldn't be done. A man like Bill Neal didn't let a challenge like that lie.

At the time, the Fraser Hotel symbolized the rough and restless male energy of a re-born mining town. On weekends the downtown of Cobalt was full of shoppers and the Fraser Hotel was always full of miners spending their pay and looking to blow off steam.

"The Fraser Hotel was always full," recalls Georgie Church. "The men sat on one side and the women sat on the other. A woman could never go into the men's side. They drank alone. A man could go over and sit with the women. But you never went over to his side."

The artificial division between the men and women was part of a divide that extended through most of the social and family life of the community. The mine crews worked six days a week and, when the Saturday shift finished up in the early afternoon, the miners would head straight to the Fraser House. "The men would go drinking on Saturday afternoons and when they'd come home around 5:30 they'd often be too drunk to go out again," recalls Georgie Church. "So we'd leave them at home with the kids and get dressed up and go out on Saturday night. You'd have to get there around 7:30 if you wanted a seat."

At the Fraser Hotel, live music was a must. "Entertainment was always a big thing. There was this one guy who was up on the stage singing when the owner walked up and said to him, 'Do you know you're fired?' He asked. 'I dunno', the singer replied, 'Hum a few bars and I'll see'."

For youths like Peter Larabie, the big entertainment on a Friday night was sitting across from the Fraser Hotel and watching the fights. "We used to sit in a little stairwell at the Staedleman Apartments across the road and we'd watch the fights at the Fraser. They used to throw guys through the doors; the windows would be breaking. People would come flying out into the streets. It was just like in the movies."

Lorie Church has been a bartender at the Fraser for many years, and she is well aware of the reputation the Fraser had in her youth. "My mother and Georgie would go down there every Friday night waiting for the fights to start. My grandmother would say, 'You'd better not go down there, there's gonna be trouble'."

Tales are still told about one particularly rough bunch of brothers, the Cobalt equivalent of the Black Donnellys. "You'd think there was a thousand of them the way people used to talk about them," Lorie muses. "I think even the cops were afraid to come to town because of them. They were good-looking men, but they were awful characters. Their sister killed a man once. Shot him right in the head."

"Although Cobalt was a tough place," explains Peter Larabie, "so were Timmins, Kirkland Lake, and Sudbury. These places were unbelievable. I guess they were just typical mining towns. It used to be the big thing to drive up to Rouyn to fight. They used to fill carloads of local guys to go up there and fight. I remember the first dance I went to was a Teen Town dance at the Community Hall. Some of these guys came over from Quebec and a big fight broke out. One guy pulled a knife and Garry

Soucisse had to jump through the second story window of the Community Hall to get away."

Doug McLeod worked as a bartender for many years at the Miner's Tavern up the road. He believes that the memories of big barroom brawls are greatly exaggerated. "Sure, there was the occasional scrap," he says, "but all this talk about going up to Rouyn to fight is crazy. If you were going to go up to Rouyn to start a fight, you'd have to bring a goddamn army with you."

One oldtimer explained the protocol of local fighting: "If you and me were going to get into it, nobody interfered; not the cops, not your best friend, no matter if I was putting the boots to you. We settled our own score."

Peter Larabie explains that even small-town toughs were expected to be polite to older people. "If we were hanging out on the street and older people were walking by, we'd move out of the way. We had respect for older people. Things were different then, you know. Like if the cops came to break something up and they took you home, you stayed there. They didn't need to go around charging people with things 'cause most people listened to them."

Georgie Church underlines this point with a story of one group of enterprising characters who took to stealing ground from the graveyard and selling it as topsoil: "Somebody came over to the Fraser one night and said there was a body uncovered in the graveyard. Nobody believed them, but we went over to have a look and sure enough, there was a head sticking out of the ground."

After the culprits were found, they were let off with a warning. "Of course they never got charged with anything. Nobody got charged back then."

"Cobalt never worried very much about the police because we took care of our own problems," explains Marta Leopold. "One time when we were about eleven or twelve, we were out walking and we saw this guy sitting in his car at the side of the road exposing himself. My girlfriend said we should go right home and when we got there she picked up a knife. We go out and there he is again. She leans in the car and says, 'See this? If you keep hanging around here you won't have anything left to play with.' We never saw him again."

Taking care of their own problems was part of the legacy of growing up in a frontier town. It was manifested in the town's willingness to take care of its own misfits and malcontents. Just as people didn't rely on the police to settle their disputes, they rarely looked to professional social workers to deal with the people who fell between the social cracks. Marta remembers some of the odd characters who inhabited the local terrain of her childhood.

"There used to be a guy," she remembers, "who walked the railway tracks everyday. I think he had been shellshocked in the war. He'd talk to us and nobody would ever bother him. One time we saw him howling at the full moon just like a wolf. If that was today, he'd be locked up. But most of these people back then lived with their mothers."

Locals talk fondly of local characters like Joe Crutch, Morgan the remittance man, or Magoo, men who weren't shunned or handed over to the dubious care of professionals. On the back roads of Cobalt there remained recluses and possibly the deranged, who lived in shacks and wandered into town occasionally.

Cobalt still has a wonderful tolerance for those who might be outcasts in other communities. In bigger centres it is easy for these individuals to be marginalized or ignored. Sometimes, in some ways, small towns like Cobalt simply have more room.

CHAPTER TWENTY

Searching for
the High-Grade

*When I was nineteen I was married and had two children. We moved into
an apartment in Paul Macmillan's building and we used to hear voices
and noises at night. I thought it was haunted at first, but it was the sound
of the men working down below. The sound would carry through the rock.
We'd hear the voices right in our bedroom.*

– Freeman Smith (talking about Cobalt in the early 1970s)

A RMAND COTÉ came home to Cobalt in 1954. After years of working in
the mining camps of the Porcupine, Quebec, and the Maritimes, he
took a job as a mine captain at the reborn Nipissing-O'Brien operation. Agnico Mines had emerged as a prime developer in the region and Coté eventually became superintendent of all of Agnico's activities in the Cobalt camp. Agnico
succeeded in the Cobalt camp because its operations were small and flexible. The
company moved its crews from property to property trying to locate likely deposits of
silver. Over the thirty-five years that Coté worked in Cobalt, Agnico reopened many of
the old properties.

To succeed in these scavenging operations, Agnico relied a fair bit on the judg-
ments of its front line troops—the underground miners. The level of trust and responsibility the company placed in its workers is notable, yet without this approach,
mining would probably have not been profitable. "The only way to keep mining profitable in Cobalt was to keep the stopes as narrow as possible. You had to eyeball it a lot.
Nobody could tell you how many ounces of silver a vein would run, and so the men
got good at judging themselves what was ore and what wasn't."

Coté believes that because the town was small and the operations limited, the
company was able to develop a good understanding with the men they were sending
down.

You got to know your workers not only at work, you got to know their families, their wives. You knew where they lived. In the bigger mines you never knew who the men were on the other shift. You never got to see them. You go to a big mine and they put you on a job that you might be on for the rest of your life. In a big mine, you've got the pipefitters to put the pipes in, the track layers to put the track in, the timbermen to just put in timber. But here, you were expected to know every aspect. That way if you needed to, you could send a man to do anything; timber, mining, drilling, laying track or pipe, whatever. Our drift crews would put in their own track, their own pipe. Our men did everything. And that is why you have so many good miners coming out of this town.

After retiring from Agnico in the early 1990s, Coté looked back on his life underground: "I am thankful that I was able to work with some of the finest people you could find anywhere. If I had to do it all over again, I wouldn't change anything."

While Agnico kept its head above water by relying on a number of properties, Dr. Norman Keevil found success in Cobalt with just one, the Silverfields. As president of Teck Corporation, Keevil optioned the old Alexandra property just south of town in 1962. Exploration proved the property viable and the Silverfields Mine came into production. Silverfields became the largest producer in the camp through the 1960s and remained on the scene for twenty-one years.

Maurice (Mousy) Mercier gained his first experience in mining at Silverfields. "I guess the mines are an obvious choice when you have no education," he says matter-of-factly. "I never even finished my grade eight because my Dad died and I had to get out and find work. I had just turned seventeen when I started at Silverfields. I worked there for seventeen-and-a-half years."

Natural geology favoured the Silverfields operation. The success of the mine came from a good balance of high grade silver and the steady milling of lower-grade ore. There wasn't much ground to work, only a claim and a half, but Silverfields made the most of it. "It was in an old river bed," explains Mousy Mercier. "I guess that when the silver flowed upwards, the ground was faulty being that it was a river system and the silver flowed into it. They had some real good silver veins, like the stope we had on the fourth level. It looked just like jewelry when you washed it down. It just sparkled."

Mousy Mercier remembers Silverfields as a good company to work for. "They had such great teachers, men like Armas Pelletier and Cliff Perry. They were slow, methodical, and they did things to perfection, and when you're working underground that means a lot. I wish I could take everything they knew and put it in my head. They knew more than all these new shift bosses put together."

In 1966 an open-pit iron ore operation started in Temagami. Sherman Mine was perhaps the closest thing this region has had to a large-scale industrial operation. Employing over three hundred men, Sherman relied on big-scale excavation and heavy production quotas to stay in business.

The blasting of ore was done by long-hole drilling, which brought down massive amounts of rock off the sides of the pit. These were gathered up with giant steam shovels with seven- and eight-yard capacities and put into the backs of dump trucks equipped to carry loads of eighty-five tons each. A large plant that converted the ore into pellets was built, and each year over a million tons was shipped south to the steel mills of Hamilton.

Dick Hunter organized Sherman and Adams Mine (Kirkland Lake), along with a number of the small silver-mining locals for the Steelworkers. He had joined the union in the bad old days of the Kirkland Lake strike and remembers how labour relations began to change by the 1960s.

The role of the union has changed from the depression days. Management used to fight the union on everything. Then in the 1960s we began to see a different attitude coming from management. Instead of constant confrontation it became a matter of negotiating. If the boss goes out and tries to impose something on the guys, he's got a confrontation. But if he goes to the union staff representative and says, "Look, we signed a contract with you guys, now we want you to produce," it becomes the union's job to make sure things get done. It became a matter of constantly negotiating with one another—you look after this and we'll look after you. If you did, they would give you small concessions.

Miners working in the 1960s and 1970s faced conditions that had greatly improved since the early days. Gone were the days of the lowly paid workers who were known to be "cheaper than timbers." In the years after the war, miners became higher paid as the companies came to rely more on skill than brawn. The incentive to big production came from the bonus paid to the workers. It made mining very lucrative to men willing to work hard, but it also tempted men to take short cuts on safety.

Health and safety underground had improved greatly since the early days. And yet, the work remained violent and threatening in nature. Each generation of miners has its own tales to tell of the war that is waged for minerals. Mousy Mercier remembers one of the accidents at Silverfields:

One of the guys I worked with, Louie Samson, was driving a raise up one time. He blasted the day before and then went up at the start of his shift to take another section out. He was banging on a steel pin when the wall gave way on him. He had come up alongside an old stope that no one knew anything about and it was full of muck. This was fine muck, though, thank the Lord, and it started to run out beneath him but he held onto that steel. He was a hundred and some feet up in the air and finally the muck filled the raise up to where he was. If he hadn't of been holding onto that steel he would have been dead.

The bosses come along and see what's happened so they started mucking him out. I don't know how many hours they dug but Louie shut out his light and he waited. He could hear the guys talking "Are we going to find him? Where's his body?" And when they got close enough that he could see their lights, all of a sudden he let out a bellow and I'm sure they almost died of a heart attack. He was a pretty funny guy.

It's too bad, but he died at the mine a few years later. He got buried in alive when the ground gave way beneath him. When the ground gives way like that at the mine they call it getting buried in a chimney. He dropped down twenty-five feet and the muck just covered him. When they found him, his hat was still on him and it looked like he was trying to climb out when it started to crumble inwards and buried him. He had twelve kids and I think his wife was expecting the baker's dozen when he died.

Cobalt has escaped many of the tragedies that have hit the bigger camps, but there has always been a slow, steady attrition—back injuries, eye injuries, men getting their arms ripped off in the mill. According to the Ham Commission on Mine Health and Safety, during the period 1970-74 Cobalt had the second highest average of non-fatal injuries in the mines of northern Ontario. These accidents and maimings rarely killed a man, but they ended many careers.

As Mousy Mercier states, "A lot of guys got crippled here from this and that. You didn't really notice it at Silverfields because we had what they call light duty. If a guy gets banged up he goes on light duty. So you didn't really notice the loss. There's a lot of guys crippled today because of the mines."

The mechanization of mining has decreased work-related fatalities, but it hasn't necessarily meant a decrease in accidents or illnesses. There are many young and strong men who have returned to Cobalt from work in other camps after being permanently sidelined from the workforce because of work-related injuries.

There is also the issue of toxicity in the mining environment. A 1994 report filed by the Industrial Disease Standards Panel has concluded that many factors are responsible for the statistically higher cancer rates in hard-rock miners. Exposure to radon gas, silica dust, diesel fumes, and known poisons such as arsenic, chromium, and cyanide are part and parcel of the miners' trade.

Arsenic is the principal component of the cobalt and nickel ores found in the Cobalt ore bodies, and the treatment of this deadly byproduct has always been problematic. In the refining process, arsenic fumes were trapped in ventilation bags as the fumes were being drawn into the smoke stacks. When these bags filled up with arsenic, men had to go in and remove them. The job was known as "cleaning out the baghouses," and it was treacherous. Men hired to do it were not supposed to work more than fifteen minutes out of an hour at this job because of the toxicity levels of arsenic.

Unfortunately, arsenic poisoning is cumulative—it never leaves the body. Men who are exposed to it are continually raising their toxicity levels. To this day, mining operations remain exempt from provincial health standards on arsenic exposure. One local miner, working in a gold operation, was told to slap Aqua Velva on his face to keep the arsenic burns down. A local nurse remembers dealing with men at the hospital who were brought in with bad cases of arsenic exposure. "You could always tell the burns from the refinery because it looked like they'd been burnt from the inside out."

One former employee of the refinery remembers the danger of the arsenic:

> I went to see Dr. Dunning one time because my eyes were swelling up so much that I couldn't pry them open in the morning. He said to me, "In ninety-nine years you'll be dead and gone, but those arsenic spots, they'll still be in the coffin right where your eyes used to be. Why don't you quit that job?"

Many men who work under these conditions do so with mixed feelings— despite the possible hardship there is a deep love and respect for the work. The attitude of many women is less ambiguous. Although the mine pays the bills, it represents a constant threat. In the early days, this fear was directed towards the ringing of the nine whistles, but in more modern times it stems from the dreaded phone call.

For Verla Moore, the feared phone call came in the middle of the night. At the time, she was a young mother of three daughters. Her husband Eddie was working the night shift at the Temagami Copperfields Mine. One night the company phoned to say he had broken his back at work. He hasn't walked since.

Marta Leopold was working in the kitchen at the local hospital when she received the phone call informing her that her brother had been injured at a gold mine in Wawa. He had been scaling loose when a piece of rock the size of a Volkswagon fell against his ladder, crushing him under it. "I was working at the hospital in the kitchen and I remember standing there holding the tray and it just flew right out of my hand. For no reason. I knew right away, that something bad had happened. Right after that, they said I was wanted on the phone. And that's when they told me about my brother."

The women in mining towns know the bitter fruits that can accompany the big pay of underground miners.

"I have always worried about Mousy working underground," says Emily Mercier, "every time that phone rang I thought, Oh, oh. If he was late I would start worrying. You just never know." Mousy shrugs it off. "Ah, you get used to it, just like anything else. Lots of other guys have close calls in their work. Cops have close calls. Construction workers have close calls. Everybody has close calls."

"You've had many a close call, kiddo," Emily replies.*

---

*At presstime we learned that Mousy Mercier had been seriously injured in September 1996 in an underground accident at Detour Lake Gold Mine.

CHAPTER TWENTY-ONE

Every Mother's Mistake

My father left home when we were young to go running with the carnivals. He didn't come back very often, but when he did the whole town would know it, especially the cops. He'd park down by the station in a little van giving out stuff from the midways like toy poodles and giving all the kids a buck. It used to burn my mother's arse. She'd say, "Jesus Christ, he's gone for three hundred and sixty-five days and he's coming back to town like he's a king giving everybody a buck except us."

– Marta Church Leopold

I N 1966 Peter Larabie grew his hair long and joined a rock'n'roll band. Dreams of Elvis were giving way to the magic of the Beatles. "I was sixteen years old. I started playing music with Eddie De Gagne, Steve Malick, and Steve Brown. We were called Every Mother's Mistake. We had paisley pants and coloured shirts. We were the long-haired individuals of the town and were lacking in the standard Elvis haircuts that everyone had. To tell you the truth we were disliked pretty much everywhere we went."

But once the band got their chops down, they began to gig throughout the region. "We played everywhere you could think of, every small nook and cranny, or Legion Hall. We even played in the bush in Gogama for ten Indians. We started with the Beatles and the Dave Clarke Five, and then as it went on into the seventies, it just started getting heavier—Jimi Hendrix, Cream. That's when we started to roll."

The hotels in northern Ontario didn't hire rock'n'roll bands in the sixties. The older crowd didn't like it. The order of the day was country and western. Things quickly changed at the beginning of the 1970s, when the drinking age in the province was lowered from twenty-one to eighteen. "Suddenly," recalls Peter, "the hotels wanted rock bands. It was like a mad panic." They became the house band at the

Tri-Town Motor Inn. The gigs were steady and the crowds were always big.

Being part of the local music scene allowed Peter to experience more counter-cultural influences than many other teens had access to. One of the big influences at that
time came from the influx of hippies from American cities. In the 1970s, northern Ontario, like many places in Canada, faced an influx of Americans escaping the war in
Vietnam. Many settled in the backwoods of Kenabeek and Charlton (some forty-five
minutes up the road). The draft dodgers pushed the parameters of social convention.
Peter Larabie remembers their influence:

> A lot of draft dodgers moved up along Elk Lake Highway. They were all excellent
> people, and some were very good musicians. There's still a lot of them living back
> there. We used to go out to where they lived in Kenabeek. What a trip! One time,
> Eddie and I drove out to this guy's place and there's this big black girl driving a
> tractor and she's got no top on! You just didn't see things like that around here.
> We then went into the living room and this girl comes down with no clothes on!
> The guy who lived there acted like it was no big deal. I'll tell you, we used to rock
> out there.

For most teenagers in Cobalt, things were a little more subdued. The big source of entertainment for Marta Leopold was going uptown to hang out at the Deluxe Grille.

"We used to hang around the Deluxe Grille. We'd order shoestrings, which were a
form of french fries. We'd get a big plate of them for thirty-five cents. I used to wear
bell bottoms then. I had a pair of peacock blue ones that I bought at Buckovetsky's. I
think I paid $1.25 for them."

"The Deluxe," explains Helene Culhane, "was really grungy inside. It was just
wonderful. We used to hang out at the Deluxe and bum cigarettes from the owner,
Jack Chow. 'Hey Jack, gotta smoke? Hey Jack, gotta smoke?' He must have had to buy
them by the carton because we were always bumming them. We'd go in there and
none of us ever had money to blow. We'd go down, have a pop and smoke a pack of
cigarettes."

A major preoccupation, naturally, was the opposite sex.

"In grade nine and ten we hung out in Haileybury," says Helene Culhane,
"because the Haileybury boys liked the Cobalt girls and the Cobalt girls liked the
Haileybury boys. The Cobalt boys liked the Haileybury girls and the Liskeard girls.
We did not date each other. Very rarely did you date one of your own, because growing
up so close knit it was like we were all brothers and sisters. I dated only Haileybury
boys."

And yet important events like dances and proms were still something that was
done at home. "Even though I went to high school at ESSM (Ecole secondaire Saint
Marie) in New Liskeard, I did the proms at the high school in Cobalt. There were

buses available to go to the dances up there, but it didn't feel like it did here at home. I don't remember what I wore to my prom but I remember what my date wore. He wore a brown shirt and a brown tie and a brown suit with brown pants, brown belt, brown socks, brown shoes and not one brown matched. I remember that very, very, very clearly. I didn't walk in proudly, but I walked in."

These were the years when the top ten singles chart dominated a teenager's social life. In the age of the CD and video, the power of the single has been very much eroded. But in the seventies, the forty-five rpm was king and the singles chart set the rhythm and moods for teenagers. A popular place to hear the latest songs was down at the arena in the winter.

"We used to buy forty-fives," recalls Marta, "and whenever we'd go skating we always had the good ones to play. The arena had really good forty-fives and we'd just go there and skate around for a couple of hours. One of our gang bought a Barracuda after working for Morissette's diamond drilling and we used to drive all around Cobalt on a dollar's worth of gas. Sometimes it would be even less. Most often we would park at the Deluxe and meet the other kids. We'd hang around and talk about bands."

In the early 1970s the biggest band in Canada was the Guess Who. On one of their tours they came to Cobalt to play at the arena. On the way up to Cobalt, the band bus broke down on the highway at the Cobalt Truck Stop. As a member of the local rock aristocracy, Peter Larabie and his group rushed out with their van to pick up Canada's biggest rock stars.

"I got Burton Cumming's signature on my arm and swore I would never wash it again," remembers Marta Leopold. "He talked to us and seemed very nice."

Lorie Church sums up her brush with fame: "Yeah, we were so close he spat on me."

Just as children used the mine shafts to play in, the teenagers in Cobalt used them for romantic rendezvous or for parties. While their younger brothers were riding down the ice-filled open stopes in the summer on crazy carpets, the older ones were going to the shafts for drinking parties. "All of my peers started drinking at a very young age," says Helene Culhane. "Some started in grade eight, but most of us were drinking by grade nine. We drank cheap wine. My first drunk was on wine. The four of us went splits on it and spent the rest of the night in the bathroom throwing up. It was a really good time. My mother only caught me drinking once. I came home from this party and it was in the winter and winter in Cobalt means boots. I come from a family of seven children and that means many boots. I tripped over one of them and my mother smelt me on the way down."

One of the choice spots to drink was on the old mining properties. Some used the open shafts as places to keep the beer cold. Others positioned themselves on the far side of the open cuts to discourage any adult from coming after them. Marta remembers one time she was up on the old Coniagas property:

> When I was in about twelve or thirteen, Dwight Bridges and I went up on Blueberry Hill to have a drink. All of a sudden we heard a cry . We rushed over and a guy had fallen down the mine shaft. So we went over to the fire hall and told them what happened, but they didn't believe us because we've been drinking. Then we went over to the Deluxe and they weren't going to do anything either. That's when I started to cry. Someone said, "Well, if you want anything done, you'd better go back to the fire hall and cry to them." The thing is that since we were only twelve and were drinking, we knew we'd be in for big trouble. So when we saw that fire truck heading out to help the guy we knew that we were now in big trouble. We didn't care whether that guy lived or died.

Cobalt in the early 1970s was a town that believed it had thrown off the mark of tragedy. A number of projects were undertaken in the first half of the decade that showed the growing sense of interest the community was taking in its past. The town toyed with many ideas about promoting the community as a tourist destination. Throughout the early '70s, a team of people chronicled buildings and areas in Cobalt as part of a larger plan to develop the tourism potential of the area. The Cobalt Restoration Committee was interested in preserving the authentic nature of the mining camp.

Plans for the downtown included renovated shops along Lang Street and a restored vaudeville theatre. Then, as now, there was the struggle between those who saw the old properties and headframes as menacing eyesores, and those who believed they were part of a unique historical fabric. Still, there were high hopes riding on the project. It would be a long-term investment in the rejuvenation and growth of the community.

But as the spring of 1977 unfolded, the optimism quickly turned to despair. In a single afternoon, the dreams for a better Cobalt vanished in the heat and smoke of a devastating fire. Cobalt was about to be plunged into its worst disaster yet.

CHAPTER TWENTY-TWO

Struck Down by Fire

What is Cobalt most famous for?
The fire.
When was the fire?
May 23, 1977.
How did the fire start?
It was started by a cigarette that fell out of a building.
It started the grass on fire. My grampa saw the fire.
Before the fire, Cobalt was like a big city. But after the fire everybody left.
Will you live in Cobalt when you're old?
No.
Why not?
There's nothing here.

> – A history of Cobalt according to the grade five class at Saint Patrick's
> School.

THE VICTORIA DAY WEEKEND: the chance to put behind a long winter and relish the prospect of another hot summer. In northern Ontario it is time to get the boats out of storage and into the water for the opening of the fishing season. The young people call it the "May two-four weekend," in reference to the first big outdoor party of the coming season.

Victoria Day, a Monday in 1977, fell at the end of three weeks of abnormally hot weather. In the morning the temperature had already risen to twenty-seven degrees Celsius and the winds were blowing above thirty miles an hour. Reg Osterberg was relaxing with a beer in the backyard of his house on Lang Street. Across the road, Lucy Damiani was beginning the spring planting in her garden. Over on Earle Street, Mousy Mercier was getting ready to go fishing. He never made it that day. "Shithouse luck," he says, looking back.

Verla Moore was in her kitchen when one of her daughters rushed in to tell her there was a fire in the downtown. Verla shrugged. Something was always burning in

Cobalt; why should she pay any attention this time? People were used to seeing the old mining properties go up in flames, or watch decrepit shacks succumb to bad wiring, arson, and careless smoking. In recent years, fires had claimed many of the local landmarks—Tressider's Red and White and Charlie Ferris's Boston Grill.* The fires always drew a big crowd.

The fire that Verla's daughter had noticed was in the abandoned Rowden building on Lang Street. The old Knights of Columbus building beside it was an equally rickety old eyesore. They seemed fated to burn.

Ed Cook had come that weekend all the way from Mississauga, Ontario, hoping to make salvage money by tearing down the Rowden and the adjacent Knights of Columbus hall. The job wasn't going well, so he sent for his son Paul and nephew Stephen Fraser, who were both sixteen, to come up on the bus and help with the work. It was about to become a lot more troublesome than he ever dreamed.

After taking a cigarette break, Stephen tossed his butt into the debris that was piling up behind the building. Before anyone realized what was happening, there was smoke billowing out of the pile. It burst into flames and in no time at all was out of control.

"You see," explains Reg Osterberg, standing on the empty lot where the Rowden building once stood, "they had taken off the roof and left the walls. When the fire started, it created a chimney effect. It was just like a woodstove going up."

As soon as the smoke was spotted, the local Cobalt-Coleman firefighters rushed onto the scene. Some were in gear, some were still in their street clothes. With the arrival of the first two trucks, they hurried to get water on the flames. But there wasn't enough water pressure in the hydrants. It was a bad sign of things to come.

It had just passed 12:30 p.m., and the men were struggling to contain the growing blaze. The Rowden building, the Knights of Columbus hall, and the Doire home were engulfed in flames. Eddie Lavalleé and Ed Labelle were working a hose when flames shot across the road burning their hose and igniting Osterberg's second-hand store and apartments on the other side of the road.

A vacant lot (the scene of a fire in the 1950s) separated the Doire home from Damiani's Furniture store and residence. Lucy Damiani was on her knees in the backyard, engrossed in planting her new garden, when she began to notice that the wind had suddenly picked up, becoming hot and dirty. When she glanced up she saw a rising curtain of fire.

By this time the call had gone out to firehalls in Haileybury, New Liskeard, and Dymond township. Men began rushing in from their cottages and fishing boats to don their gear and head to the growing blaze in Cobalt. The fire was now leaping north

---

*Some locals like to tell the apocryphal story that owner Charlie Ferris only allowed the firemen in to fight the fire if they promised not to touch the candy.

along Lang Street and the intense heat and wind were creating fireballs that whistled through the air, igniting homes.

Mousy and Emily Mercier had just finished lunch when they saw the flames and smoke coming towards them. "The fire began jumping," recalls Mousy, "and started coming down to where we lived. Then the firemen came and said, 'Get out, you gotta get away from here.' I got up on top of the roof with a two-inch fire hose and I stayed there 'til the firemen chased me off."

Emily remembers how quickly they were caught up in the nightmare. "The fire was only two houses down from us and the wind was blowing towards us. I was taking a fit because instead of getting out of the path of the fire, Mousy was trying to fight it. I was running around shouting, 'Get Mousy off the roof! Get Mousy off the roof!' Then Porky Watters, one of the New Liskeard firemen, came along and said, 'Get the hell off that roof, Mousy, you dummy'."

While some just stood and watched in amazement, others rushed to save what valuables they could. Many in the immediate path of the fire moved their belongings up the road, believing the fire would not continue spreading. Some old people were unwilling to leave. Others were in shock and disoriented. Meanwhile the fire kept moving, claiming houses, cars, trees, and yards full of furniture.

Peter Larabie remembers how his family were forced out. "My dad opened the cupboard and poof! The flame came through like a blowtorch. It burnt his face and clothes. He said, 'Let's get out of here.' My brother came running out of the house and the only thing he had was a pot [marijuana] plant. He was trying to save it. My mother said, 'Why are you wasting time with those stupid plants, when there are more important things to save?' She didn't know what it was. This thing was like a tree. She was trying to save the silverware and he was saving his pot plant!"

Peter Larabie spent the day helping people get their belongings out. "Me and a couple of other guys were using my father's old green pickup truck to take stuff out of the fire area. But by the end, the fire was going right through to the end of town, so we went to my place across the lake where we could watch it. The heat was so intense you could feel it on the other side of the lake."

Once on the other side of the lake, he realized that his most precious possessions had been left behind. "We were sitting up on top of the pickup watching the fire burn and I was thinking, 'Thank God, nothing of mine is caught over there'. Just then I realized that I had lent this guy my organ and my Leslie speakers. He had my Hammond organ, my Hohner piano, and my two Leslies. It was over in a garage across from Ste. Thérèse Church. Do you know how long I saved up for that equipment? I used to play for a hot hamburger after a gig. All the rest of our money went to buying equipment. The two Leslies came from [the band] Steppenwolf. I even had them autographed by the band. It was my pride and joy. I just freaked. All that mahogany wood must have burnt so well."

He wasn't the only one to lose a prize possession. "Jean Louis worked for months and months on the drills in South America to be able to buy a brand new gold Jaguar. He put it up on blocks for the winter and didn't have any insurance on it. He was going to come back for it in the spring. It burnt. What a beautiful car."

Emily Mercier was trying to stem the spread of the fire by throwing buckets of water on sparks that fell in the yard. "You'd look up in the air and hear this whistling sound," she recalls, "and there would be a big ball of bloody fire. Anything it would hit would just start to burn. The whole house would be in flames."

Her husband Mousy had joined the ranks of men, many clad in t-shirts and shorts. "There was a house right where the old-age home is now and it was a real hot spot. I was there for two hours and we were shooting water on it and it didn't burn. We saved it, then they turned around and tore the goddamn thing down. If I had known that, I would have let the bastard burn."

As the afternoon wore on, people lost their sense of time and their sense of fear. Women and teenagers from the unaffected section of town made their way through the scattered ranks of volunteers with sandwiches and refreshments. People sorted out fire hoses, relayed messages, and grabbed hoses as they became available.

By mid-afternoon, the fire was working its way through the little streets of French-town. Driven back by heat and a lack of water, the firemen watched helplessly as the fire moved in on Ste. Thérèse Church. They were stunned to see the parish priest come out and kneel in front of the church. At first it seemed as if he were going to be devoured in the inferno, but the fire moved around the church, leaving the building unscathed. Indeed, it destroyed a house right behind the church and then veered out and around the convent next to it. Both church properties remained standing, while all around them was obliterated.

Reg Osterberg remembers the situation at the church. "When you've got nine fire departments running at the same time, the system can't handle it. We ran out of water. We drained everything. I remember seeing the priest kneeling in front of the church praying. The heat up there was unreal. It was something that you wouldn't believe unless you saw it."

Peter Larabie has often thought about the way that Ste. Thérèse was spared.

"The church didn't burn. There wasn't even a mark on it. Mrs. Whatchamacallit's house in between the church and the convent burnt, but the church buildings didn't. Everyone kinda takes it for granted that it didn't burn, but when you think about it, it's pretty strange. There's gotta be something there, guys, so let's get it together."

Up in Haileybury and New Liskeard town officials were coordinating emergency radio to help the crews in Cobalt. The hospital was on alert preparing for the deluge of victims they feared would be coming in from the fire zone. The Haileybury arena was opened to begin receiving furniture brought from the evacuees.

The fire crew at Sherman Mine was called by CB because the phones were down.

Firemen across the lake in Quebec had seen the flames and rushed over to help. Already, pieces of burning debris were being carried by the wind into North Cobalt. A small brush fire had started out near the cemetery. If the fire succeeded in crossing over into Mileage 104, the firefighters knew they would be fighting the fire in Haileybury by nightfall.

Phone service and hydro power was out. Verla Moore's cousin in North Dakota had been phoned by relatives about the fire, and when she tried phoning Verla the operator told her, "You can't get through to Cobalt. It's burning to the ground."

Those who were watching the fire from the other side of Cobalt Lake saw the arrival of the water bombers. From the edge of the fire zone, they slowly worked their way in. By suppertime the fire was in retreat and the crews began to work their way through the streets, snuffing out the flames that had broken down into individual fires.

As the fire died down, the extent of the calamity began to sink in. Mayor Bruce Lonsdale, only twenty-seven at the time, called an emergency meeting with town councillors and officials from the nearby communities. They began assessing the damage. The issue of restoring of water, hydro, and phone service, as well as providing food, shelter, and clothing, had to be dealt with immediately.

Emily and Mousy Mercier had taken refuge with their young family at his mother's place on Hudson Bay Road. Emily remembers looking out from the safety of this home over the devastation below. "I stayed up half the night, just staring out there. It was awful. All the hydro was down and it was dark, just like a nightmare. That night when you looked out, you never thought that people would even think of rebuilding. You never thought people would have the courage to start over. It was mass destruction."

Georgie Church joined others from the south end of town who went up to see what had happened in French town. "At night we walked through the fire zone and met all kinds of people we knew who had been burnt out, and they had no idea where they were staying. Everything was down, except the church. It was so sad. Just like a bomb hit it."

The devastation in Cobalt became national and international news. Journalists arriving on the scene were shocked by the devastation. A writer from *Reader's Digest* arrived and immediately set about trying to secure interviews with the exhausted firefighters. One of them said, "I'm in no mood to talk, I just lost my whole fucking town." In all, 459 people were homeless and about 140 buildings destroyed. A quarter of Cobalt had been levelled in an afternoon.

"When we walked through it the next morning," says Mousy, "it looked like the moon. It looked like Sudbury, just barren all around and rock."

The army brought in a soup kitchen and families who had been unaffected gave countless hours in volunteer work. The nearby towns supplied large amounts of toys, clothes, and furniture for the victims. Although many had lost their homes and property, it was a miracle that no one had been killed. The hospital had treated cases of shock, burns, and lacerations, but the spectre of death had thankfully passed them by.

People remember the first days after the fire as having a kind of special grace. Cobalters remember the goodwill of the nearby towns. "The people of New Liskeard were on the scene first," recalls journalist John R. Hunt. "The day after the fire the mayor of New Liskeard came down with a cheque for $10,000. He came to me because he couldn't find anyone else and said, "What the hell should I do with this?" I said, "Well, let me take you to the Legion and buy you a drink."

Despite the often acrimonious relations between the three communities in the Tri-Towns, the help Cobalt received has never been forgotten. "You've never seen people pull together like they did after the fire," explains Mousy Mercier. "The Tri-Towns are like that. We'll tear each other's throats out, but if something happens, we bond as one. Once it's over, we're back to tearing each other apart. But after the fire, you couldn't ask for better people."

The rebuilding of Frenchtown took place, with austere square bungalows on larger lots replacing the tumbled housing that had made up the old neighbourhoods. People talked of building a better Cobalt, of having the opportunity to turn around the slow decline of the community. In the years to come, however, the real damage of the fire became clear. As John R. Hunt states, "The fire destroyed an extraordinarily interesting community within a community. It was the French and Italian neighbourhood. I used to love walking through those streets. There was a very strong French-Canadian community and association that used to play a big role in the Miners' Festivals. They used to stage entertainments and things like that. When the fire swept through Frenchtown, it seemed to destroy that community spirit. There was a great shifting as neighbourhoods were broken up. And that great sense of community was gone."

Over the next number of years, when the mines began to close and downtown business began to atrophy, the memory of the fire hung heavily over the community. There are many reasons for the decline of Cobalt in the 1980s and early 1990s, but there is no escaping the fact that something of the great Cobalt spirit was lost in the flames. In local memory, the fire marks a great divide between the world that existed before Victoria Day, 1977, and the world they have lived with ever since.

3

Picking Up
the Pieces

D O I WISH *that my children will be able to stay here when they grow up? No. Having the young leave is the way it's always been here.*

– Marta Church Leopold, local nurse

My husband says that the tumbleweed will be blowing down the street and we'll be the only ones left. But we're not leaving. I love this place.

– Helene Culhane, Cobalt town councillor

CHAPTER TWENTY-THREE

The Longest Decade

After the fire the town just couldn't seem to get itself back on track. The stores started to close and the young people began moving out, but I think it was the fire that really took the wind out of people's sails.

– Jackie St. Laurent, retired school principal

THE MINERS' FESTIVAL falls on the first weekend in August. An influx of tourists arrives annually, drawn by the novelty of hand-mucking and jack-leg drilling contests held down at the arena. Over beer and hot dogs, people sit up in the dusty temporary bleachers watching local miners show off their skills. Twenty years ago, the Festival was a rollicking twelve-day affair. Now it is a modest four-day festival, but the smaller crowds still have a good time. The Miners' Festival weekend is the highlight of the year in Cobalt, when the prodigal children return to take stock of the town they left behind.

During the Miners' Festival in 1992, the last grocery store went out of business. It didn't come as a shock. Its empty aisles and painful bare windows drew only a casual resignation from a populace grown used to defeats and closures. George Van Altena, the owner of the Miner's Market, decided to go out in fine style. He cleared the store of stock and shelves, hired a band and put on a bash. For two nights the last grocery store in Cobalt did killer business as a dance hall.

The closing of the grocery store capped fifteen years of steady decline. Smaller fires in the years following 1977 took out what was left of many of the old Lang Street buildings. A long and bitter fight to keep the local high school was defeated, and local teenagers were soon being bussed up to New Liskeard. Cobalt, which had once been the toast of the north with its busy downtown, now resembled a ghost town, as consumer dollars continued moving out of the community and up to the burgeoning strip mall at the north end of New Liskeard. The small shops of Cobalt were no match for the shopping mall or the fast food franchises.

The closing of the last grocery store came on the heels of the last mine closure. By 1988, the silver operations of Cobalt had pretty much been put out of business by low prices and high costs. In 1990 the open-pit iron operations at Sherman Mine (Temagami) and Adams Mine (Kirkland Lake) closed. Since the mid-1960s these two mines had been a major source of economic stability in the larger area. Although there was still ore in the pits, Dofasco could get cheaper ore elsewhere. In an area with a working population of only eight thousand, eighteen hundred primary jobs and twelve hundred spin-off jobs disappeared in the years after 1988. Local estimates hinted at an unemployment rate of 30 - 40 percent.

The decline of Cobalt in the 1980s reflects the inevitable fate of resource-based towns. Sooner or later, the ore must run out, or a cheaper and more bountiful supply found elsewhere. But the decline of Cobalt in this period is as much about the drain of local services as it is about the price of ore. Even when the big boom collapsed in the 1920s, the local downtown still remained active. People still had to buy groceries, doctors still had to be seen, supplies had to be purchased. The downtown of Cobalt might have suffered, but it wasn't decimated. This was because people spent their money locally.

But the collapse of the late 1980s is reflective of the collapse of the modern rural economy. Even with the mines running, the merchants were slowly dying out. The loss of stores and services isn't unique to Cobalt. It is a struggle that is being fought across rural Canada as communities compete for services, school dollars, shopping, and economic investment. The shift towards centralization and homogenization of services has pushed small communities like Cobalt to the fringe. The battle for rural communities has become much bigger than the battle to keep a local plant or mine afloat. It is a battle over where people buy their shoes cheapest and which schools will educate their children.

Helene Culhane has grown up with this struggle. When she was going to school in the 1970s, the Roman Catholic School Board began bussing students at Ste. Thérèse school to a larger school in Haileybury. "I was in the first class bussed out of Cobalt. It took a few years, but gradually they took one grade at a time. They had grade six, seven, and eight and then they took our grade ones because we didn't have enough and they said, 'Well, we'll borrow your grade ones this year because there isn't enough to make a class and there aren't enough in Haileybury. But next year when you have grade ones you can keep them.' Of course next year the battle was lost before it was begun. My parents went to bat then, and then I had to go to bat when they were taking my children."

Over time the French-language grade school was closed and so was the Cobalt-Haileybury high school. The battle to save the high school was emotional and spirited, but according to some, it was doomed from the start. Local newspaper reporter John R. Hunt believes the school closures had a very negative affect on the town.

"Cobalt High School was closed by an ongoing and continuous blackmail attempt by one municipal council that eventually forced the Board of Education to give way. They weren't interested in saving money. What they wanted to do was get those students spending money in their town. One would have to be blind, naive, and stupid not to see it. The effect of this bussing can be seen. A lot of the young people have grown up in this town with a sense of defeatism."

Jackie St. Laurent began teaching in Cobalt in 1956. She believes the value of a small-town school cannot be replaced by larger, more distant institutions. "The mentality today is that bigger is better. This was the issue when the Hall-Dennis Report came out with big centralized boards, centralized schools, big gyms, and big libraries. They say they'll be able to provide everything for these children, but you still need the individual attention. Whereas if you have a lot of students you don't have the time for each individual student. I believe that we (in Cobalt) gave them the tender, loving care they needed. The self-esteem aspect is very important and it's there in a small town."

Equally damaging to the sense of local pride has been the loss of the local downtown. "We used to have so many stores," long-time residents are quick to state. They list the names of department stores that served residents for decades. The department store was a central feature of small-town life. The local merchant fulfilled a role similar to doctor or dentist in the local scene. All of this seems out of place in an age where shopping has become simply a hunt for bottom line price — something that can be delivered in antiseptic bulk by big American chains.

And yet, just as consumer patterns have changed since the early days in Cobalt, the merchant class has changed as well. As John R. Hunt points out, "One of the characteristics of these pioneering merchants is that they always wanted their children to do better than they did. Many of them were Jewish or Syrian and their children became lawyers or doctors. When the old man died or retired, the children sold the stock because often they couldn't sell the stores. The second and third generations weren't interested in standing behind counters for hours serving customers."

Cobalt shoppers no longer are served by the like of Sam Buckovetsky or Mrs. McDiarmond. Today their needs are met by WalMart, McDonalds, and a host of other highway franchises on the north side of New Liskeard. Better selection perhaps, but a limiting of local identity.

Just as the identity of a town is affected by the vitality of its schools and stores, it is very much marked by the kind of work available. Without a solid economic base, Cobalt has become more dependent on the "mail-box" economy. With many of the young working families having moved away in search of steady employment, it is more and more dominated by retired couples and younger people on welfare or unemployment insurance. The cultural divide between these two groups is striking. The older people resent what they see as the passivity of the welfare class.

As one old timer puts it, "When these old mining towns go on the skids, many with ambition get up and go. Lots of those who remain just don't have what it takes to make a move. In the old mining towns accommodation is cheaper and welfare perhaps easier to get, so it tends to attract a different kind of character. It was different during the depression, because you had a lot of people in the community who weren't afraid of work."

Mousy Mercier is one who has noticed the change in spirit. "When I was growing up here there were still three or four mining properties going. Cobalt was one big family. I'm not saying that Cobalt is any better than anywhere else, but Cobalt is a mining town. In a mining town everyone is friendly. They don't care who you are, what colour you are, or where you are from. But now it's no longer a mining town, it's becoming a welfare town."

John R. Hunt speaks for the disgruntled oldtimers who believe that the spirit that kept Cobalt alive is being lost in the general malaise of welfare dependency. "When I came here, most people here saw Cobalt as a very exciting place to live, a very funny place to live. Let's face it, most of them have moved away or died off and the people who have moved in since then don't have that sense of spirit. There's a bitchiness in Canada today and it's reflected here. I just wish I was younger or wasn't so blind. I think I'd head to northern Alberta or northern B.C. Those places remind me of Cobalt in the '50s. There's still some sense of hope, some sense of adventure."

There are many young people who have followed Mr. Hunt's advice and have moved away in search of work. They head to Toronto or to industrial outposts like Norman Wells in the Northwest Territories. Every mining camp from the Yukon out to Voisey Bay has at least one Cobalter working the diamond drills or hauling ore. In time, some of them come back, just as their parents came back from working in the mines of Yellowknife and Timmins. Some leave behind good jobs to try their luck amongst the slim job opportunities of home. Why do they come home? Some say they just miss the sense of community. Others say they miss the land.

In a culture that has moved increasingly to judging issues according to economics, the return of people to a town like Cobalt makes no sense. But people come back because it is home. They feel the rich fabric of family and identity is missing elsewhere. As Freeman Smith says, "The one thing about Cobalt is that you're part of a big family. In hard times you have somewhere to go. It's not like in the city where if you have a million dollars you've got friends, but if you're down and out you're on your own. Here everybody knows one another."

If towns like Cobalt are to survive into the next century, this strong sense of place will be one of its drawing cards. Small-town Canada offers lifestyle benefits that are increasingly scarce in larger centres—a sense of security, a relaxed pace of living, a sense of belonging. It provides the unique geography of local memory. Helene Culhane is one of those who believes that the sense of place should not be underestimated.

We're going to grow again, there's no question about it. The seeds have been planted, it's just going to take some time. My daughter loves this town. Sure, she says it's boring sometimes, but that's a generational thing; it's the Nintendo world talking. You see, it's the heart of this place that makes it so important. I just hope more people learn to see this. It would break my heart to see my children leave.

CHAPTER TWENTY-FOUR

Once It's Gone

A mine is like you or I, it starts to die the day it's born. Every ton you take out of it is one ton closer to depletion.

– Mike Farrell

I N 1994 a small cobalt-producing operation started up in the region. Two old mines were de-watered and a small processing plant was built. With a rise in the price of cobalt, EGO Resources was gambling on the hunch that deposits of economically viable cobalt could still be found in the old silver mines. The operation is a modest one. Thirty employees will hardly turn back the tide of past closures. But to locals, size didn't matter. Just the sight of a couple of miners coming off shift and into the Legion for a glass of draft was like seeing sunshine after years of rain. Oldtimers at the bar would press the men for details—Who got hired? Who are the stope leaders? Who got the job of pounding the ore on the grizzly? There is nothing, it seems, that old men in Cobalt like to talk about more than hauling ore and blasting muck.

How viable is a long-term mining operation in Cobalt? It remains to be seen. Any new metals operation has to compete with mega-giants like INCO in Sudbury or Kidd Creek Mines in Timmins. These operations process millions of tons of ore a year. The costs of mining are paid in copper, zinc, or nickel. By-products like silver and cobalt are basically free profit. A mine in Cobalt doesn't have the benefit of a large ore body that can be mapped out and developed over years. It's hard to attract investors when one can't guarantee more than six months of reserves in advance. The ore in Cobalt is elusive, trapped in narrow veins. Exploration is a blind and expensive game of hit-and-miss.

Since the veins are narrow, the ore has to be very rich to make mining worthwhile. Larger base metal deposits like Voisey Bay can be mined in bulk. In Cobalt, however, costs have to be kept down and very little is put into development infrastructure. The mines tend to differ little from the operations of the 1940s, relying on jack-leg drills and small mucking machines, where big mines today would use multiarmed jumbo drills and large scoop trams. The ore has to be pushed up the drifts on one-ton ore cars that have to be hauled to the surface to dump and then sent back down.

With the price of silver down around five dollars an ounce, the money to invest on unproven hunches just isn't there. Carlo Chitaroni believes that for mining in Cobalt to be profitable, the price of silver per ounce would have to be in line with the hourly wage for a miner. "Silver needs to be up around fifteen to twenty dollars an ounce to be worth mining. In the early days silver was seventy cents an ounce but wages were only thirty-five cents. If an ounce of silver was double the hourly wage of a miner today, it would be fifty dollars an ounce. Mines would reopen here. But as it is, silver isn't worth mining."

The metals market has become a global affair, with more and more Canadian companies moving their focus to untapped sources in the Third World. The recent rise in the price of cobalt ore is a direct result of instability in Zambia and Angola. And yet in spite of this instability, exploration and investment dollars continue to move toward nations like Guatemala and Chile. Mining companies have set the standard for the modern global economy, superseding notions of border and region in the pursuit of corporate profits.

In order to compete, North American mines are moving toward higher production, using ever increasing levels of mechanization and automation. The trend is toward assembly-line style production. Where other generations had to be skilled at reading the grains of the rock and knowing how to set up the right series of drill sequences, the young miner of today is more likely to be trained on computerized jumbo drills and remote control scoop trams. When skilled and difficult work is needed, many companies rely on special contract workers rather than their own crews.

The changing face of mining has changed the way miners see their work. As Mousy Mercier points out, "A lot of the work done today in the big mines is by contract workers. The contractors take on a lot of the exploration work. Most of the young guys (in these operations) don't think they're capable of that kind of work. Well they are, but they are from a younger generation and they think this kind of work is beyond them. When they see jack-leg drilling and roof bolting being done, the young miners say, 'but that's hard work. Forget it.' They aren't from the old school. It's really a shame."

It is clear that without the higher level of productivity that has been made possible by technological change, many Canadian mines just wouldn't be able to compete with the cheaper and newer mines of the Third World. What is also obvious is that changes in drilling, blasting, and stoping have made mining a safer occupation and lowered the terrible health costs that came from extracting minerals.

But the question that is harder to answer is, what future is there for the culture of work that has grown up around mining? Is the small, tightly knit mining community

with its almost feudal allegiance to the local mine going to be replaced by a more mo-
bile, uprooted team that is bussed or flown in from all over? Can the old ways of underground skill, decision making, and technique compete with large-scale production
methods?

In many ways, the miners of the north are like the Atlantic fishermen. The days of
the small boats and trawlers were deemed too uneconomic to compete against the big
draggers and the floating factories. Ore bodies in the north are being depleted at an
ever-increasing rate and the discovery of new deposits is dwindling. Gone are the days
in towns like Timmins and Kirkland Lake where a man might work his whole life in
one mine. Indeed, gone are the days when his son and his grandson would be able to
work at the same operation.

Operations are continually downsizing, retiring men in their fifties and hiring only
those with many years experience. The effect can be felt at the local cash register.
Mining jobs provide northern communities with high-paying and high-spending jobs.
Where else can a man with a grade eight education make $60,000 a year? These men
know that they aren't ever going to see nearly this kind of money learning WordPerfect
at the local high school.

More than an issue of wages, however, is the sense of pride in a young workforce
able to earn its living in the mines. It comes across in the gear, in the jargon, and in
the distinctive leather hockey jackets that every miner casually but proudly wears.
The jackets carry the crests of an exploration company, drilling team, or a mine. The
men wear these jackets, not with a sense of strutting machismo, but with the self-
assuredness of veterans. Any unemployed guy hanging out at the bar stands a little
taller because he carries the crest of "Renabie Gold," "J.S. Redpath," or "Falconbridge Exploration." But this strong sense of male self-identity has been fractured by
layoffs, downsizing, and depleted ore bodies. A young workforce is not gaining its
apprenticeship underground; it is being excluded from the cohesive identity of the
fathers.

One of the most difficult things for dying mining communities to deal with is the
loss of this sense of self. Local business leaders talk about finding alternatives to the
boom/bust cycle, but sustainable economic alternatives are hard to come by. In the
face of the unknown, people tend to clutch at what they know. Mike Brooks, a local
businessman, has been a major force in trying to find alternatives to the boom/bust
economy. He believes the rich history of the region would make Cobalt a prime
tourist attraction. Mike sums up the superstition that somehow there is always one
more major deposit lurking, one more mine to keep things going. "I don't know how
you explain to people here that a non-renewable resource is just that—once it's gone,
there's no more."

But mining lore is based on the notion of hope against all odds. The longer the
shot, the bigger the payoff. It's a throwback to the desperate luck of the gambler—an

archetype of the early mining cultures. The roll of the dice has given the mining industry its greatest dramas and most exhilarating victories. And unfortunately, many sad
defeats. For every example of the longshot paying off there many more of the luck running out. "Look at Silver Centre," says John R. Hunt. "It was a thriving little town. And
today you couldn't even find an outhouse there."

The fate of Silver Centre is the spectre that haunts all mining communities. Mining towns are notoriously poor at attracting other kinds of business.

"One of the characteristics of a mining town," explains John R. Hunt, " is that it is
considered heresy to suggest that one day the ore might run out or one day the mines
might close. I was saying twenty years ago exactly the same thing I was saying twenty
years before that, and that is that we had to begin developing some new businesses and
some new enterprises. I remember being stopped by one of the leading mining men of
the district, a very nice fellow, but he gave me supreme hell. He said Cobalt had always been a mining town and always would be; they didn't need me running around
saying we had to find anything else. Now of course the mines are all closed—with the
present prices of silver and the present environmental laws they will never reopen."

And when mining money leaves, very little remains. "Look at Coleman Township," says John Gore. "It used to be the richest township in all of Canada because all
of Cobalt's mines were there. And what have the people in Coleman got to show for it
all? Nothing! There aren't even any sidewalks or paved roads."

Mike Farrell believes that the collapse in Cobalt is merely the shape of things to
come for other mining towns.

"When I came up north about a year after the war, Kirkland Lake was a vibrant little mining town. You could see a guy walking on the street with a lunch pail in his
hand twenty-four hours a day. Kirkland Lake got its Adams Mine, which extended its
life by twenty-five years, and Timmins got Kidd Creek Mine, which extended its life
by twenty-five or thirty years. But one day Government Road in Kirkland Lake will
look like Lang Street in Cobalt. And as for Timmins, I really don't like to say it, but
what are the chances of finding another deposit like Kidd Creek? A million to one?
But the prime example of all this is Cobalt. The money was taken out of there and the
same thing has happened in Timmins and Kirkland. Until workers understand these
things, nothing is going to change. Workers aren't stupid, but sometimes they're pretty
darned naive."

But as it has been since the beginning, the hills of Cobalt are still being searched
by prospectors who believe the bonanza will return. Ralph Benner, now in his eighties, continues working on a property in the Cobalt area. He is convinced it will yield a
major mine, one that will harken back to the early boom days. John Gore, now retired,
spends his days working on an old deposit in Silver Centre. Gino Chitaroni, a third-
generation mining man, is convinced that out there under the ground that has been
picked over a million times, another great treasure is lurking.

When Jim Ireland, the resident geologist of Cobalt, was asked if he thought that anything of value could still be found, he shrugged: "We have a lot of scientific instruments and a lot of scientific theses to draw on, but it is still largely luck. Sometimes you have to throw the hammer at the fox."

Conclusion

When I go up the street I see all those old buildings that used to be shops.
They have that quaint Cobalt look and I think how they would make
beautiful boutiques and shops. There could be chocolate shops or candle
shops. All kinds of things they could be if they were restored and not left
to fall down. I just think that people would come here to see this town
where the houses are all squished in together and shaped so odd. There's
the rocks and the water, the houses and the mine shafts. There is so much
to see here.

– Linda Hall, local shopkeeper, 1993

O N A WARM NIGHT in June of 1994, the town of Cobalt threw a party. It was a gala really, complete with a smattering of evening gowns and tuxedos and the pleasing sounds of a cello to welcome the guests. In preparation for the party, planters of red geraniums were strung along the bridge leading into town. The twisting road through town, which had just come through three years of renovation, never looked so good. The iron fences, a town trademark, were given a fresh coat of blue paint and for the first time proper sidewalks connected the town from one end to the other.

The party was a celebration of the reopening of the Classic Theatre. After twenty years of decay, the old theatre was back. The Town Council, when faced with the prospect of tearing down the empty sixty-year-old building, decided instead to develop it into a modern theatre for dramatic performances. With a stagnant local economy, building a live-theatre venue struck many as a long shot. "No one will come to Cobalt to see a run-down old theatre," said the skeptics. But over the winter of 1993, the restoration of the building began, and the expectations of even the most optimistic were quickly surpassed.

Two of the designers of the Winter Garden Theatre in Toronto, Richard and Claire Smerdon, were smitten with the project and offered their services. Restoration of the building fell on the shoulders of Paddy Puhakka, the town carpenter, and his crew, many hired by government grants from the ranks of the unemployed. The money for the project was limited, the aims great. Paddy and his crew worked with dedication, and over the course of the winter, the building was transformed into a modern, functional, and beautiful site.

When the theatre opened, people were taken aback by its beauty. Here, in a town that many had given up for dead, was a state-of-the-art, live-theatre venue with plush seats, a large stage, and a proper lighting and sound system. Visitors were welcomed into a mezzanine with a large oak staircase and glimmering chandelier. On the smoked glass above the main doorway was a beautiful etching of the town of Cobalt from an era when theatres were all the rage.

The rebuilding of the Classic Theatre symbolized a new era in the community. It was as if people were finally ready to put the memory of the fire and the mine closures behind them. The time had come to start a new chapter.

Once the theatre was completed, though, the questions of the skeptics remained. What was the town doing spending money on building a theatre when the local economy was in tatters and the population unemployed? But what else could be done? Realizing that the days of waiting for mining money to restore the economy was over, the town had to begin making decisions about its future.

There are those who believe that the great battle has been lost. They believe that the old Cobalt is no more and people should be content being a bedroom community for New Liskeard. Such a view maintains that Cobalt is just another random gathering of dwellings, a town no different from any other dotting the highways of Canada. But it is no such thing.

The visual geography of the place defies dismissal. Every summer, artists from across Ontario descend on Cobalt to paint pictures of the narrow streets and old headframes. The attraction of artists for Cobalt goes back to the days of the Group of Seven. The town is a living landscape of odd shapes, colours, and winding terrain. It speaks of another time and another way of seeing the world. In a culture being increasingly fed on bland esthetics, the landscape of Cobalt defies suburbanization.

Culturally, the community also defies easy categorization. Even casual visitors are struck by the fierce sense of common memory. Old buildings may have burnt down, many families may have left but they continue to be present in the minds of the residents. When people describe streets or landmarks, they often refer to buildings that have disappeared as though they were still there. A few years after moving to Cobalt, someone asked us if we had met Tommy Black. We had heard many stories of the old store owner, but assumed he had been dead for decades. "Oh he's dead all right," the man replied. "I'm just wondering if you'd met him yet."

There are many keepers of the stories. Retired ironworker Doug McLeod is one of these. When we approached him for an interview, he chased our tape recorder away as if it were a mickey of alcohol smuggled into a Presbyterian church. Yes, he would be more than happy to bring back to life the people he knew and share with the listener all their foibles and eccentricities, but he would steadfastly guard their dignity from graverobbers and curio hunters. He stood before us in his battered fishing hat and blue workshop coat like a gatekeeper of the dead. We had to understand that in writing a history of Cobalt we were not simply gathering up lore and legend: we were gathering up lives.

It draws to mind the story told by Alexander Carmichael about his journey through the Hebrides and Highlands of Scotland in the late 1870s, collecting the oral traditions of the Gaels. He related how one night an old man recited to him a beautiful bedtime rune. After Carmichael left, the man followed him twenty-six miles to plead that he not write the poem down in a book. "Think ye," said the old man, "if I slept a wink last night for thinking of what I had given away. Proud, indeed, shall I be, if it give pleasure to yourself, but I should not like cold eyes to read it in a book."

The investment in the Classic Theatre makes perfect sense when one considers that locals have always put great value in this elusive power of ghosts and memory. Theatre exists in the imagination and has always had to fight for its place in a world that judges only the bottom line. While the long term implications of this theatre cannot yet be gauged, it is apparent that the Classic Theatre is already transforming the cultural horizons of a young generation of Cobalters. When plays come to town, the local urchins often fill the front rows. They sit with their eyes wide open, taking in the magic of the stage. Many come without their parents, leaving their pieced-together bikes in clumps outside the side door. They come to cheer on live theatre because it is there.

Helene Culhane is one of those who felt her faith in the community restored by the rebuilding of the theatre. When asked if she thought the old Cobalt spirit was dead she responded, "Oh God, it's alive and growing. It has been growing even more since the rise of the phoenix—the theatre. I think the theatre just awakened so many people who were sleeping. Some of them are groggy and are still waking up. It's wonderful. When I walk into the theatre I just get goose bumps. The town is coming back. You can feel it taking on a life of its own."

Whether or not economic revitalization will come to one of Canada's unique frontier towns remains to be seen. But clearly Cobalt cannot be judged in terms of whether it is viable in a post resource-based world. The town has survived a century of wild promise and bitter defeat. It will no doubt survive into the next century. The economics of ore extraction has not been able to overshadow the love people have for this place with its meandering streets, its restless ghosts, and its wonderful sense of home.

So when you see our tar-paper shacks and the shapeless, rough lumber buildings, do not say, "How ugly, and what a horrid-looking town." Think of the high hopes, the brave hearts, and the strong hands that built them.
    – Elizabeth MacEwan, Cobalt's first schoolteacher, 1955

Chapter Sources

Chapter 1

For a good discussion of early silver discoveries, see D.M. LeBourdais, *Metals and Men: The Story of Canadian Mining* (1957); Michael Barnes, *Fortunes in the Ground* (1986); Roy Longo, ed., *Historical Highlights of Canadian Mining*, pp. 66-88; H.V. Nelles, *The Politics of Development*, pp.108-53; and Alexander Gray, "Genesis and Revelation of Cobalt," The Toronto *Globe*, 3 October 1908; also see "The Davis Handbook of the Cobalt Silver District," *Canadian Mining Journal* (1910); *Ontario Mines Handbook* (1906); and John Murphy, *Yankee Take-Over at Cobalt* (1977).

A background on the Klondike Gold Rush can be found in Pierre Berton, *Klondike: The Life and Death of the Last Great Gold Rush* (1958); Douglas Fetherling, *The Gold Crusades: A Social History of Gold Rushes.* (1988), pp. 149-94; McKinley and Darragh's experience mentioned in John Murphy, *Yankee Take-Over at Cobalt.* (1977), pp. 4-11.

George Woodcock quote cited in Douglas Fetherling, ibid., p. 10.

Chapter 2

Account of the early days in the Cobalt camp see: Elizabeth MacEwan, "Early Days in Cobalt," unpublished speech presented to the University Women's Association (1955). Cobalt Mining Museum Archives, Cobalt, Ontario.

Information on William Trethewey came from Ben Hushes, "The Trail of the Prospector," Toronto *Globe*, 3 October 1908: p.3. (The entire 3 October issue of the *Globe* is devoted to mining in the early Cobalt camp.)

For early mining myths and reference to Agricola's work see Kathleen Briggs, *The Vanishing People* (1978), p. 83.

Chapter 3

Sources from Elizabeth MacEwan, "Early Days in Cobalt" (1955); also Anson Gard, *The Real Cobalt: The Story of the Great Mining Camp* (1908) and *Silverland and Its Stories* (1909).

Sources on the silver rush to Cobalt: John Murphy, *Yankee Take-Over at Cobalt* (1977);

Douglas Fetherling, *The Gold Crusades* (1988); Louis Kurowski, *The New Liskeard Story* (1991); and Edmund Bradwin, *The Bunkhouse Man* (1972).

For Frank Cowdery, see "Letters from Old Timers," Cobalt Concentrates, 50th Anniversary Issue (1953), p. 17.

Hans Buttner letter from Letters to the Editor, *Daily Nugget*, 11 December 1909.

For information regarding the orderly nature of the Cobalt camp, see "No Need for Fantastic Statements When Describing Cobalt's Big Era," Cobalt Concentrates, 50th Anniversary Issue (1953), p. 8; Frederic Robson, "Cobalt: A Mistaken Idol." *Canadian Magazine* , vol. 1, no. 2, 1908. Also interviews with Charlie Dean and Alfred Parent (7 April 1972) .

Regarding bootlegging in the Cobalt camp, see Maude Groom, *The Melted Years* (1971); also Editorial, "Blind Piggers and Pinkertons," *Daily Nugget*, 2 January 1911, p. 2; and *Daily Nugget*, 20 January 1911.

For sources on the amount of ore, see: *Twenty-Five Years of Ontario Mining History: A Review of Outstanding Developments in the Last Quarter of a Century*, bulletin no. 83, Ontario Department of Mines, 1932; *The Daily Nugget*, 3 January 1910; "Early Strikes were Fabulous," Cobalt Concentrates, 50th Anniversary Edition, (1953); and *Daily Nugget*, 3 January 1910, p. 1.

Mention of bordellos in Cobalt in Maude Groom, *The Melted Years*, and Dan Hellens,*The Cobalt Connection*. Information regarding prostitution in Kirkland Lake camp from Andre Wetjen and L. Irving, *The Kirkland Lake Story* , p. 70; in Timmins, see A.E. Alpine, "Timmins, Yesterday and Today," *The Northern Miner*, 28 March 1994.

Chapter 4

Father John O'Gorman quote from the *Eganville Leader*, 9 May 1906.

For information regarding development in Cobalt, see Michael Barnes, *Fortunes in the Ground*. See also Toronto *Globe*, 3 October 1908; Frederic Robson, "Cobalt: A Mistaken Idol," *Canadian Magazine*, June 1908; Douglas Fetherling, *The Gold Crusades*; John Murphy, *A Yankee Take-Over at Cobalt*.

Millionaires' row is mentioned in Albert Tucker, *Steam into Wilderness* (1978).

For a good discussion of the laws concerning mining and taxation, see H.V. Nelles, *The Politics of Development* (1974), pp. 154-81.

The draining of Cobalt Lake is discussed in Douglas Baldwin, "The Development of an Unplanned Community: Cobalt 1903-1914," Plan Canada (1978); H.V. Nelles,*The Politics of Development*, pp. 168-72.

Chapter 5

Mrs. Holden from "Cobalt's Grand Old Lady Plans to Enjoy the Fun," Cobalt Concentrates, 50th Anniversary Edition (1953), p. 20.

Sources for the life of women in the camp are: Elizabeth MacEwan, "Early Days in

Cobalt"; Maude Groom, *The Melted Years*; general information available in Elizabeth Margo, *Women in the Gold Rush.*

For the housing difficulties in Cobalt, see Douglas Baldwin, "The Development of an Unplanned Community: Cobalt 1903-1914"; Douglas Baldwin, "A Study in Social Control: The Life of the Silver Miner in Northern Ontario"; Toronto *World*, 1 April 1906, p. 18; Town of Cobalt Council Meeting minutes, 15 January 1907, 1 December 1907, 13 January 1908.

For information pertaining to the role of the TN&O in the development of the early mining communities, see Albert Tucker, *Steam into Wilderness*; Douglas Baldwin, "The Development of an Unplanned Community: Cobalt 1903-1914"; H.V. Nelles, *The Politics of Development* (1974), pp. 154-81.

Information on the early schools from Elizabeth MacEwan, ibid., pp.20-21.

Chapter 6

Quote from Frederic Robson, ibid., p.100.

Information on sanitary conditions in Cobalt camp from: Douglas Baldwin, "Public Health Services and Limited Prospects: Epidemic and Conflagration in Cobalt," (December 1983); also Douglas Baldwin, "The Development of an Unplanned Community: Cobalt 1903-1914" (1978); The Sanitary Journal of the Provincial Board of Health, Annual Report, 1905; Elizabeth MacEwan, ibid.

Town of Cobalt Council minutes relating to issues of sanitation: 15 January 1907, 17 May 1907, 23 May 1907, 15 September 1907; pigs and cows running through streets of town: 21 March 1907, 15 April 1907; need for a town cemetery: 3 July 1907, 19 February 1908, 10 February 1908, 31 July 1908.

Sources of information on public lavatories: Maude Groom, ibid; Douglas Baldwin, "Public Health Services and Limited Prospects: Epidemic and Conflagration in Cobalt"; Town of Cobalt Council minutes, 19 March 1908, 13 March 1909.

Source for information on the Coniagas dispute with the Jamieson Meat Market: Douglas Baldwin, "The Development of an Unplanned Community: Cobalt 1903-1914."

Background information on fire-related concerns: Douglas Baldwin, "The Development of an Unplanned Community"; Elizabeth MacEwan, ibid.; development of fire by-law 89 from Town of Cobalt Council minutes, 23 May 1907, 19 February 1908, 7 July 1909, 21 July 1909; according to the *Daily Nugget*, 13 July 1911, the town had a very good first six months with only twenty-six fires.

Quote from public health nurse cited in John Murphy, *Yankee Take-Over at Cobalt* p. 24.

Concerns over hospital facilities in the camp were raised during the Town of Cobalt Council minutes on 5 March 1907, 20 March 1907, 6 October 1907 and 16 May 1908.

Information regarding the draining of Cobalt Lake from Douglas Baldwin, "The Development of an Unplanned Community"; H.V. Nelles, ibid. pp. 167-71.

Chapter 7

Sources on ethnic diversity from Maude Groom, ibid.; Douglas Baldwin, "The Development on an Unplanned Community: Cobalt 1903-1914"; also conversation with Cobalt resident Doug McLeod (summer of 1993).

Information on the social growth of Cobalt from Douglas Baldwin, "The Development of an Unplanned Community: Cobalt 1903-1914"; "Banks so Busy Windows Used as Entrances," reprinted in Cobalt Concentrates, 50th Anniversary Issue (1953), p.12; also the Cobalt Mining Museum Archives provided an excellent collection of photographs, newspaper clippings, and articles on the early social life of Cobalt.

Cobalt the Dog stories from John Macfie, "Before the Fire: A Memoir of Early Hailey-bury," based on interviews with his mother, Edith Macfie, between 1980-84; also from Cobalt Mining Museum Archives. Cobalt the Dog t-shirts are still a big hit with tourists to this day.

Sources on sports: interview with Gerald McAndrew (18 May 1972); Scott and Astrid Young. *O'Brien: From Water Boy to One Million a Year* (1967), pp.58-74; for slightly differing interpretations of the Cobalt Silver King rivalry with Haileybury, see John Murphy, ibid., and Leslie McFarlane, *A Kid in Haileybury* (1975).

On growing gold fever, see Douglas Fetherling, *The Gold Crusades* pp. 211-30; Michael Barnes, *Fortunes in the Ground* , pp. 85 -190; Michael Barnes, *Gold in the Porcupine!* (1975); Roy Longo, ed., *Historical Highlights of Canadian Mining*, pp. 88-101; L. Carson Brown,"Kirkland Lake — 50 Golden Years," pamphlet reprinted by Canadian Geographic Society, 2d ed., June 1970; "The Song of Gold has Replaced the Song of Silver," The *World*, 19 November 1911; head-lines from the *Daily Nugget* dominated by staking news from the Porcupine throughout 1911.

Chapter 8

Opening quote from Mike Farrell, 9 July 1993.

Source for Millionaire's Row: Albert Tucker, *Steam into Wilderness* (1978), p. 42; even today the line of houses along Lake Timiskaming in Haileybury remains among the most im-pressive in northern Ontario.

For sources for union battles in American context, see Mike Solski and John Smaller, *Mine Mill: A History of the Mine Mill and Smelter Workers* (1985), pp. 1-18; Stewart H. Holbrook, *Rocky Mountain Revolution* (1956); John Murphy, *Yankee Take-Over at Cobalt* (1977), pp 91-98.

Information on early union organizing among Cobalt miners from Bruce Hogan, *Cobalt: The Year of the Strike 1919* (1977); Mike Solski and John Smaller, ibid., pp.55-70; John Murphy, *Yankee Take-Over at Cobalt* (1977), pp. 91-108; W. H. P. Jarvis, *Trails and Tales in Cobalt* (1908); also information from interviews with Jack Rauhala (9 May 1995), Bob Carlin (14 April 1991) and Jim Tester (15 September 1988).

Information concerning the Keeley Mine disputes and the collapse of the Farmer's Bank from: the *Daily Nugget.*, 19 January 1911.

Hearings of the Royal Commission of Inquiry into Industrial Relations in Canada, Cobalt, Ontario. May 1919.

For information on the formation of the Algonquin Unit, see G.L. Cassidy, *Warpath: The Story of the Algonquin Regiment 1939-1945* (1990), pp.1-44.

Chapter 9

Opening quote from Leo O'Shaughnessy (March 1972).

From Ontario Department of Mines Annual Report 1910. (Accident reports are published yearly in the Ontario Department of Mines Annual Reports.)

Quote from Bronte Svekers (12 February 1972).

Information on mining techniques from: *Mining In Canada*, 6th Commonwealth Mining and Metallurgical Congress, 1957; W. H. P. Jarvis, *Trails and Tales of Cobalt* (1908); Douglas Baldwin, "A Study in Social Control: The Life of the Silver Miner in Northern Ontario," (1973); also based on interviews with John Gore (summer 1993), Armand Coté (1 May 1993) and Ernie Tressider (19 October 1993).

Chapter 10

Opening quote from Ralph Benner interview (spring 1993).

Sources for the story of M.J. O'Brien and the O'Shaughnessy family: Scott Young and Astrid Young, *O'Brien: From Water Boy to One Million a Year.* (1967); also based on interviews with Leo O'Shaughnessy (1972), Marvin Armstrong (May 1993) and Jean O'Shaughnessy Keating (summer 1992).

Information on milling techniques from *The Milling of Canadian Ores*, 6th Commonwealth Mining and Metallurgical Conference. General information pp.3 -90, information specific to Cobalt pp. 165-72 (1957); see also Ontario Department of Mines Annual Reports; also numerous conversations with John Gore.

Ragged Chutes information from: John Murphy, *Yankee Take-Over at Cobalt* (1977), pp. 123-38.

For information on hydroelectric development in northeastern Ontario, see James Morrison, "Colonization, Resource Extraction and Hydroelectric Development in the Moose River Basin," November 1992.

Chapter 11

Opening quote from Bob Carlin (14 April 1991).

Quote from Gertrude Underwood (16 May 1972).

For background on the development of the One Big Union, see David J. Bercuson, *Fools and Wisemen: The Rise and Fall of the One Big Union* (1978); Mike Solski and John Smaller, ibid.; Brian Hogan, *Cobalt: The Year of the Strike 1919* (1977); and interview with Bob Carlin (8 October 1987).

For an in-depth overview of the 1919 strike, see Brian Hogan, ibid.; also John Murphy, ibid., pp. 185-96.

For accounts of the problem with scabs, see Maude Groom, ibid.; and interview with Bob Carlin (14 April 1991). For references to tension between veterans and strikers, see Brian Hogan, ibid., pp. 99-132; also Dan Hellens, *Memoirs of a Miner*.

Source for decline of silver deposits in the Cobalt camp, see John Murphy, ibid., pp. 189-93.

For information pertaining to public opinion of the strike, see J. A. McRae, "Banner of Bolshevism Behind Strike of Miners in the Northern District," *Saturday Night*, 16 August 1919, p.18; J. A. McRae, "Radicals Appear to Gain Ground in Cobalt Strike," *Saturday Night*, 16 September 1919, p. 6; also good discussion of press coverage in Brian Hogan, *Cobalt: Year of the Strike 1919*, pp. 122-30, 184.

Chapter 12

Laura Landers quote from interview, March 1991.

Information on Mining Corp. from interview with Armand Coté, 1 May 1993; also Ontario Department of Mines Annual Reports for years 1920-1928.

For information on Kerr Lake and other area mines, see Ontario Bureau of Mines Annual Report; also interviews with John Gore (March 1991) and Ralph Benner (spring 1993).

For sources of information regarding the Ragged Chutes hydro project, see John Murphy, ibid., pp. 123-30; and *The Daily Nugget*, Diamond Jubilee issue, 29 July 1963.

References to declining town infrastructure from Town of Cobalt Council minutes, 11 September 1923 (sidewalks), 19 February 1924 (concern over taxes), 17 April 1923, 5 June 1923, 19 June 1923, 10 November 1923, 19 February 1924, and 8 April 1924 (welfare requests); 6 March 1924, 15 July 1924 (general infrastructure issues).

The account of Mr. Oscar Kivi comes from the *North Bay Nugget*, 21 September 1923, p.5; and Town of Cobalt Council minutes, 17 August 1923, 6 March 1923, and 3 October 1923.

Chapter 13

John Gore quote from interview (March 1991).

Account of Taffy Davis from Maude Groom, ibid.

Accounts of growing up during depression: interviews with John Gore (March 1991); M. J. Scully (3 May 1993); Joe Malick (28 February 1993) and Ernie Tressider (19 October 1993); also numerous conversations with Doug McLeod.

For information on Silver Centre, see Peter Fancy, *Silver Centre: The Story of an Ontario Mining Camp*; also Peter Fancy, *Silver Centre Re-Discovered*; interview with M. J. Scully (3 May 1993).

Chapter 14

Quote from Joe Malick interview (28 February 1993).

Information on the nature of work at this time from interviews with Joe Malick and Jim Jones (28 February 1993); Carlo Chitaroni (11 May 1995).

For source for the James Fitzpatrick reference to the Nipissing Central Railway, see Peter Fancy, *Temiskaming Treasure Trails* (1993), p. 9.

Source for information pertaining to the Yorkshire Mining Company, see Ontario Department of Mines Annual Reports, 1934.

Information on the shipping of cobalt to Germany from interview with Gerald Paul Presse (2 May 1972).

Anecdotal information on illegal drinking establishments in Cobalt from interview with Joe Malick and Jim Jones (28 February 1993).

For general information regarding the growth in the northern gold camps, see Michael Barnes, *Fortunes in the Ground*, pp. 167-222; Alexander Hellens, *Memoirs of a Miner*.

Sources of work conditions in the gold camps: Alexander Hellens, ibid.; interviews with Cuthie Dixon (3 August 1992); Myrtle MacLeod (10 April 1994); Armand Coté (1 May 1993).

Information pertaining to union activities from: Andre Wetjen and L. H. T. Irvine, *The Kirkland Lake Story*; Laurel Sefton MacDowell, "Remember Kirkland: The Gold Miners' Strike of 1941-42"; also interviews with Bob Carlin by R. Stowe (8 October 1987) and Myrtle MacLeod (10 April 1994).

For the story of INCO, see Jamie Swift, *The Big Nickel: INCO at Home and Abroad.*

Source for influx of workers into Sudbury: Industrial Disease Panel Report on Lung Cancer in Hardrock Mining (March 1994).

Chapter 15

Quote from John Gore interview (March 1993).

For an overview of the Algonquin regiment during WW II, see G. L. Cassidy, *Warpath: The Story of the Algonquin Regiment 1939-1945*; also the Bunker Military Museum Archives (Cobalt) has an excellent collection of photos, memorabilia, and articles (source for letters and information pertaining to Victor Miettinen).

Information on life in Cobalt during the war: interviews with Jim Jones, Curator of the Bunker Military Museum (28 February 1993); Ralph Benner (27 May 1972), Doug McLeod, Ernie Tressider, and Vivian Hylands (19 October 1993), and Joan Montieth (March 1992).

Edith Fowke, *Folk Songs of Canada*. (1978).

Chapter 16

Opening quote by Elizabeth MacEwan, ibid.

For information on the Silver Miller Mine, see Peter Fancy, *Silver Centre Rediscovered*; interview with Reg Doan (8 May 1995).

Sources on mining for the period, see *Mining in Canada*, 6th Commonwealth Conference on Mining and Metallurgy (1957); also Ontario Department of Mines Handbook for the years 1950 -1960; Cobalt Consolidated Annual Report (1957); also interviews with Mike Farrell (9 July 1993) and Carlo Chitaroni (11 May 1995).

Sources on the resurgence of the union in the Cobalt camp were: interviews with Reg Doan (8 May 1995), John Gore (March 1991), and Don Taylor (13 August 1995).

Information concerning Elliot Lake based on: Frank Joubin, *Not for Gold Alone*; Lloyd Tataryn, *Dying for a Living*; also interviews with Marvin Armstrong (May 1993); Reg Doan (8 May 1995), Don Taylor (13 August 1995), and Georgie Church (April 1993).

Chapter 17

Opening quote from interview with Ernie Tressider (19 October 1993)

For background on the 1950s, see David Halberstam, *The Fifties*, (1993).

Sources of information on life in Cobalt in the 1950s based on interviews with: Georgie Church (April 1993); Helene Culhane (21 August 1994); John Gore (March 1991); J. R. Hunt (4 March 1993); Vivian Hylands (19 October 1993); Joan Montieth (March 1992); Paul Oblin (March 1993); and M. J. Scully (3 May 1993).

Chapter 18

Quote from Freeman Smith interview (summer 1993).

Information for chapter based on interviews with: Georgie Church (April 1993); Lori Church (April 1993); Helen Culhane (21 August 1994); Peter Larabie (August 1993); Marta Leopold (April 1993); and numerous conversations with Doug McLeod.

Chapter 19

Opening quote from Georgie Church interview (April 1993).

Sources for this chapter are interviews with: Georgie Church (April 1993); Lori Church (April 1993); Peter Larabie (summer 1993); Marta Leopold (April,1993); Doug McLeod; also conversation with Ali Neal (summer 1993).

Chapter 20

Opening quote by Freeman Smith (summer 1993)

Information relating to Agnico-Eagle mines from: Mike Macbeth, *Silver Threads Among the Gold*; Ontario Department of Mines Handbook for the years 1950-1970; also interview with Armand Coté (1 May 1993).

Information relating to Sherman Mines from: Sherman Mine Supplement, 5 September 1968; also interview with Dick Hunter (11 May 1995).

Information pertaining to Silver Fields Mine from interview with Mousy Mercier (spring 1993).

Sources for discussion on toxicity and working conditions: Industrial Disease Standards Panel (March 1994); Report of the Royal Commission on the Health and Safety of Workers in Mines, by J. M, Ham, 1976; interview with Jim Ireland, resident geologist, Cobalt (1 March 1993); also based on conversations with several local miners.

Concerning working conditions and injuries in the mines: interviews with Mousy and Emily Mercier (spring 1993); Verla Moore (April 1993); and Marta Leopold (April 1993).

Chapter 21

The sixties in Cobalt based on interviews with: Lori Church (April 1993); Helen Culhane (21 August 1994); Peter Larabie (summer 1993); and Marta Leopold (April 1993); also conversation with Ronnie Liscombe (spring 1993).

Information on the Cobalt Restoration Project is housed in the Cobalt Mining Museum Archives.

Chapter 22

For an in-depth account of the famous 1977 fire, see Don Curry, *Fire! Cobalt: May 23, 1977*. Information concerning the fire obtained from interviews with: Reg Osterberg, Cobalt Fire Department, (spring 1992); Georgie Church (April 1993); Lucy Damiani (March 1991); J.R. Hunt (4 March 1993); Peter Larabie (summer 1993); Mousy and Emily Mercier (spring 1993); and Verla Moore (April 1993).

See "Premier Declares Cobalt Disaster Area," *Temiskaming Speaker*, 25 May 1977.

Chapter 23

Opening quote from interview with Jackie St. Laurent (March 1993).

Story of the closing down of the grocery store based on conversation with George Van Alta (fall 1993).

Sources for the struggle to maintain the local high school: interviews with Jackie St. Laurent (March 1993); J. R. Hunt (4 March 1993); and Helene Culhane (21 August 1994).

For the changing economics of the Cobalt economy: interviews with J. R. Hunt (4 March 1993); Mousy Mercier (spring 1993); and Freeman Smith (summer 1993); also conversations with Randy Gagnon and Mike Parcher (summer 1992).

Chapter 24

Opening quote from Mike Farrell (9 July 1993).

For changes in mining, see: Wallace Clement, *Hardrock Mining*; interviews with Carlo Chitaroni (11 May 1995) and Mousy Mercier (spring 1993).

Present economic realities based on conversations with Mike Brooks, town councillor and Gino Chitaroni, Prospectors and Developers Association; Jim Ireland (1 March 1993); J. R. Hunt (4 March 1993); John Gore (March 1991); and Ralph Benner (spring 1993).

Conclusion

Opening quote from Linda Hall (March 1991).

The Town of Cobalt has an excellent story board display on the state of the theatre before and during renovations. Information about renovations based on conversations with Richard and Claire Smerdon as well as then-town clerk Lorraine Brace. Also George Othmer, Mike Brooks, and Helene Culhane.

Artistic response to Cobalt from Laura Landers (March 1991).

Closing quote from Elizabeth MacEwan, ibid.

Glossary of Terms

---

assay. The testing of an ore sample in a laboratory to determine the value of the minerals contained.

ball mill. A type of mill equipment that grinds ore down into fine particles. It is a long cylindrical machine filled with steel balls. Crushed ore is fed into it as the ball is rotated. The steel balls smash against the ore, crushing them into particles.

base metal. The name given to commercial minerals like copper, iron, zinc, and cobalt. Base metals are inferior in value to the precious minerals like gold, silver, platinum, and diamonds.

blasting. In order to be able to extract the ore, a series of sequenced holes (8 to 12 feet long) have to be drilled in the rock. Some of the holes are filled with blasting powder and others left empty to allow for expansion. The miner blasts the rock and then is able to remove the valuable ore.

blind pig. An illegal drinking establishment.

bucket. A platform for lowering men underground. When a shaft is being sunk into the rock, the bucket is used to haul men and their tools down the shaft.

cage. The elevator that carries men down the shaft.

concentrate. When the waste rock has been removed in the milling process, the valuable remains are referred to as concentrates.

concentrator. A mill that separates valuable minerals from waste rock. The concentrator then has to ship its product to a refinery for the final recovery of the minerals.

cross-cut. A passageway that is constructed underground to meet the vein.

de-water. When a mine closes down, the drifts underground either fill with water naturally or are intentionally flooded by the company. Keeping the timbers underwater keeps them from rotting. When a company goes in to explore an old property, they first have to pump out the water; this is known as de-watering.

diamond drill. A hollow drill that is used in exploration work. As the drill is sunk into the ground, the hollow centre takes a continuous sample of rock. These samples are known as drill cores and are examined by geologists for possible ore values.

drift. A tunnel underground that leads out from the shaft.

face. The wall of rock where drilling is done.

grizzly. An iron grille laid over an ore chute or ore pass where rock is dumped. Rock that is too big to fit the grizzly must be broken into smaller pieces.

head frame. The building that covers the shaft. It is designed to carry the men and materials to and from the depths of the mine.

high-grade. Ore that is very rich in value. A highgrader is someone who steals valuable ore like gold or silver from a mine.

hoist. The machine that is used to raise and lower the cage in the shaft.

hoist-room. The hoist room is the small building that directly faces the headframe. This is where the hoistman runs the hoist cable which runs to the top of the headframe and then down to the cage.

jack-leg drill. A drill, usually weighing between 80 and 125 pounds, that is balanced on a movable leg. The jack-leg drill is used for drilling into the face of the rock.

level. The level is the name given to the underground passageways (drifts). The levels are set at regular intervals and are designated by their depth from the surface—1300' level, 1450' level, etc.

loose. Rock that is hanging loosely after a blast. Miners have to use long scaling bars to pry this loose rock off before resuming work. This is called scaling loose.

mill. The building where ore is taken and the valuable minerals are separated from the waste.

muck, mucker, mucking-machine. Muck is the name given to rock after it has been blasted. A mucker is the man who has to muck the ore out—either by shovel or a mechanical machine. A mucking machine is a platform attached to an ore car with a scoop on the front of it. The mucker picks up ore with the scoop and flings it back into the ore car.

open cut. An excavation of ore that is exposed to the surface. In Cobalt, the open cuts look like long, narrow caverns.

ore. Rock that has something of value in it.

ore chute. Ore is removed from a stope by dropping it down to a lower level where it can be gathered into ore cars. The ore chute is the passageway that is built to control the movement of this blasted rock.

ore reserves. The known and quantifiable amount of valuable ore that exists in a mine.

pillar. A block of rock that is left in place to hold up the ground above it.

raise. A passageway that goes up, either up to another level, or up into a stope.

refinery. The final process where valuable minerals are separated and poured into their final product.

rounds. This is a blasting term. After a series of holes have been drilled into the rock, the blasting powder is placed in them and the rounds are blasted.

scaling bar. An iron bar used to pry loose rock from a stope. The process is known as scaling.

scoop tram. The name given to the four-wheeled, diesel-run machines that are used to transport muck underground. The use of scoop trams is known as trackless mining, because older methods of mucking involved the laying down of railway tracks on which ran the ore cars.

shaft. The hole, like an elevator shaft which extends into the earth and from which the levels are run out horizontally.

silica. Silica is the name given to quartz mineral after it has been blasted and becomes dust.

skip. A bucket that is used to hoist ore to the surface.

slimes. The name given by locals to the fine green tailings that were dumped on the hillsides.

stope. The part of the mine where the mining of ore is done. It is an excavation that starts below the vein and gradually works its way up into it.

tailings. The residue of waste rock that is left over after the milling process and is dumped out onto the surrounding landscape. In some mines, the tailings are used as backfill underground. When dumped on surface, they are stored in tailings ponds because when under water, they have less of a chance of leeching into the surrounding environment.

tram, trammer. The hauling of ore cars underground. This is the job of the trammer. In the old days the cars were pushed by hand, but gradually this was replaced by motorized tramming cars.

waste rock. Rock that has no ore potential.

Bibliography

Interviews

Armstrong, Marvin. Interviewed by C. Angus, May 1993.

Benner, Ralph. Interviewed by Carmen Stubinski, May 27, 1972.

Benner, Ralph. Interviewed by B. Griffin, spring 1993.

Brocklebank, Arthur. Interviewed by Carmen Stubinski, February 19, 1972.

Brosko, Michael. Interviewed by Lucy Damiani, May 5, 1972.

Buckler, Harry. Interviewed by Carmen Stubinksi, May 18, 1972.

Carlin, Bob. Interviewed by Rick Stowe, October 8, 1987.

Carlin, Bob. Interviewed by Rick Stowe and C. Angus, April 14, 1991.

Chitaroni, Carlo. Interviewed by Charlie Angus, May 11, 1995.

Church, Georgie. Interviewed by B. Griffin and C. Angus, April 1993.

Church, Lori. Interviewed by B. Griffin and C. Angus, April 1993.

Coté, Armand. Interviewed by C. Angus, May 1, 1993.

Culhane, Helene. Interviewed by B. Griffin and C. Angus, August 21, 1994.

Damiani, Lucy. Interviewed by B. Griffin, March 1991.

Dean, Charlie. Interviewed Carmen Stubinski, 1972.

Dixon, Cuthbert. Interviewed by C. Angus and B. Griffin, August 3, 1992.

Doan, Reg. Interviewed by C. Angus, May 8, 1995.

Farrell, Mike. Interviewed by C. Angus, July 9, 1993.

Gagnon, Randy. Interviewed by B. Griffin, summer 1992.

Gore, John, Interviewed by C. Angus and B. Griffin, March 1991.

Hall, Linda. Interviewed by B. Griffin, March 1991.

Hunt, John R. Interviewed by C. Angus, March 4, 1993.

Hunter, Dick. Interviewed by C. Angus, May 11, 1995.

Hylands, Vivian. Interviewed by C. Angus and B. Griffin, October 19, 1994.

Ireland, Jim. Interviewed by C. Angus, March 1, 1993.

Jackson, David Burton. Interviewed by Lucy Damiani, April 24, 1972.

Jones, Jim. Interviewed by C. Angus and B. Griffin, February 28, 1993.

Keating, Jean. Interviewed by C. Angus and B. Griffin, summer 1992.

Landers, Laura. Interviewed by B. Griffin, March 1991.

Larabie, Peter. Interviewed by C. Angus, August 1993.

Leopold, Marta. Interviewed by C. Angus and B. Griffin, April 1993.

MacLeod, Myrtle. Interviewed by R. Stowe, January 15, 1992.

MacLeod, Myrtle. Interviewed by R. Stowe and C. Angus, April 10, 1994.

McLeod, Douglas. Interviewed by C. Angus, (numerous occasions).

Malick, Joe. Interviewed by C. Angus and B. Griffin, February 28, 1993.

McAndrew, Gerald. Interviewed by Carmen Stubinski, May 18, 1972.

Mercier, Maurice and Emily. Interviewed by C. Angus, spring 1993.

Montieth, Joan. Interviewed by B. Griffin, March 1992.

Moore, Verla. Interviewed by B. Griffin, April 1993.

Nixon, Clorida. Interviewed by Lucy Damiani, March 16, 1972.

Oblin, Paul. Interviewed by B. Griffin, March 1993.

Osterberg, Reg. Interviewed by C. Angus, spring 1992.

O'Shaughnessy, Leo. Interviewed by Lucy Damiani, 1972.

Othmer, Beatrice. Interviewed by Carmen Stubinski, April 26, 1972.

Parcher, Genevive and Mrs. Riley. Interviewed by Carmen Stubinksi, February 11, 1972.

Parcher, Mike. Interviewed by B. Griffin, summer 1992.

Parent, Alfred. Interviewed by Carmen Stubinski, April 7, 1972.

Parent, Yvonne. Interviewed by Carmen Stubinski, April 7, 1972.

Presse, Gerald Paul. Interviewed by Lucy Damiani, May 2, 1972.

Saint Laurent, Jackie. Interviewed by B. Griffin, March 1993.

Scully, M. J. Interviewed by C. Angus and B. Griffin, May 3, 1993.

Svekers, Bronte. Interviewed by Carmen Stubinski, February 12, 1972.

Smith, Freeman. Interviewed by C. Angus, summer 1993.

Taylor, Don. Interviewed by C. Angus, August 13, 1995.

Tester, Jim. Interviewed by R. Stowe, September 15, 1988.

Tressider, Ernie. Interviewed by B. Griffin and C. Angus, October 19, 1994.

Turgeon, Joseph. Interviewed by Carmen Stubinski, March 7, 1972.

Underwood, Gertrude. Interviewed by Johanna Stubinski, May 16, 1972.

Journals, Articles

Baldwin, Douglas. "A Study in Social Control: The Life of the Silver Miner in Northern Ontario." *Labour/Travailleur*, 3 (1973).

Baldwin, Douglas. "The Development of an Unplanned Community: Cobalt 1903-1914." Plan Canada (1978): 17-29.

Baldwin, Douglas. "Public Health Services and Limited Prospects: Epidemic and Conflagration in Cobalt." *Ontario History*, 75 (December 1983): 374-402.

"The Davis Handbook of the Cobalt Silver District." *Canadian Mining Journal*, 1910.

Gray, Alexander. "Genesis and Revelation of Cobalt." The *Globe*, 3 October 1908, 2.

Hellens, Dan. "The Cobalt Connection." *Canadian Mining Journal*, 97, 10(October 1976).

Ledrum, Frank. "Father O'Gorman: Days that Are Gone." Unpublished manuscript transcribed by Carmen Stubinski, 11 May 1972. Cobalt Mining Museum.

MacEwan, Elizabeth. "Early Days in Cobalt." Unpublished speech 18 June 1955. Cobalt Mining Museum.

McRae. J.A. "Banner of Bolshevism Behind Strike of Miners in the Northern District." *Saturday Night*, 16 August 1919.

McRae, J.A. "Radicals Appear to Gain Ground in Cobalt Strike." *Saturday Night*, 6 September 1919.

"Premier Declares Cobalt Disaster Area." *Temiskaming Speaker*, 25 May 1977.

Robson, Frederic. "Cobalt: A Mistaken Idol." *Canadian Magazine*, vol. 1, no. 2, 1908.

Reports

Cobalt Consolidated Mining Company. "Report to the Shareholders," 1957.

"Colonization, Resource Extraction and Hydroelectric Development in the Moose River Basin; A Preliminary History of the Implications for Aboriginal People." Report presented by James Morrison to Environmental Assessment Board Hearings, November 1992.

Ontario Department of Mines Annual Reports, 1908-18, 1920-29, 1935-38, 1939-62.

Ontario Royal Commission on Health and Safety of Workers in Mines (The Ham Commission). Toronto, ON., 1976. Ministry of the Attorney General.

Report to the Workers' Compensation Board on Lung Cancer in the Hardrock Mining Industry. Industrial Disease Standards Panel, March 1994.

Royal Commission of Inquiry into Industrial Relations in Canada (The Mather Commission). Cobalt, ON., May 1919. Microfilm 1981, vol. 2, 1747-1890.

Sherman Mine Supplement, *Dofasco Illustrated News*, 5 September 1968.

The Sanitary Journal of the Provincial Board of Health of Ontario. Annual Report. 1905.

Town of Cobalt Council Minutes from 1907-8. 1923-24.

Books

Barnes, Michael. *Fortunes in the Ground*. Erin, ON: Boston Mills Press, 1986.

Barnes, Michael. *Timmins: The Porcupine Country*. Erin, ON: Boston Mills Press, 1991.

Barnes, Michael. *Gold in the Porcupine!* Cobalt, ON: Highway Book Shop, 1975.

Bercuson, David J. *Fools and Wisemen: The Rise and Fall of the One Big Union*. Toronto, ON: McGraw-Hill Ryerson Ltd., 1978.

Berton, Pierre. *Klondike: The Life and Death of the Last Great Gold Rush*. Toronto, ON: McClelland and Stewart, 1958.

Briggs, Katherine. *The Vanishing People: Fairy Lore and Legend*. New York: Pantheon Books, 1978.

Brown L. C. *Cobalt: The Town with a Silver Lining*. Canadian Geographic Journal, January 1974.

Cassidy, G. L. *Warpath: The Story of the Algonquin Regiment 1939-1945*. Cobalt, ON: Highway Book Shop, 1990.

Clement, Wallace. *Hardrock Mining: Industrial Relations and Technological Changes at INCO*. Toronto, ON: McClelland and Stewart Ltd., 1981.

Curry, Don. *Fire! Cobalt: May 23, 1977*. Cobalt, ON: Highway Book Shop, 1978.

Fancy, Peter. *Silver Centre: The Story of an Ontario Mining Camp*. Cobalt, ON: Highway Book Shop, 1985.

Fancy, Peter. *Silver Centre Re-discovered*. Cobalt, ON: Highway Book Shop, 1987.

Fancy, Peter. *Temiskaming Treasure Trails 1910-1915*. Cobalt, ON: Highway Book Shop, 1993.

Fancy, Peter. *A Guide to Historic Cobalt*. Temiskaming Abitibi Heritage Association, 1994.

Fetherling, Douglas. *The Gold Crusades: A Social History of Gold Rushes*. Toronto, ON: Macmillan of Canada, 1988.

Fowke, Edith. *Folk Songs of Canada*. Waterloo, ON: Waterloo Music, 1978.

Gard, Anson. *The Real Cobalt: The Story of a Great Silver Mining Camp*. Toronto, ON: Emerson Press, 1908.

Gard, Anson. *Silverland and Its Stories*. Toronto, ON: Emerson Press, 1909.

Girdwood, Charles, Lawrence Jones, and George Lonn. *The Big Dome*. Toronto, ON: Cybergraphics Company, 1982.

Groom, Maude. *The Melted Years*. New Liskeard, ON: Temiskaming Printing, 1971.

Hellens, Alexander Daniel. *Memoirs of a Miner*. Don Mills, ON: Lifestories, 1989.

Hogan, Brian F. *Cobalt: The Year of the Strike 1919*. Cobalt, ON: Highway Book Shop, 1977.

Holbrook, Stewart H. *Rocky Mountain Revolution*. New York: Henry Holt and Company, 1956.

Jarvis, W. H. P. *Trails and Tales in Cobalt*. Toronto, ON: William Briggs, 1908.

Jones, Lawrence and George Lonn. *Historical Highlights of Canadian Mining*. Toronto, ON: Pitt Publishing, 1973.

Joubin, Franc. *Not for Gold Alone*. Toronto, ON: Deljay Publications, 1986.

Kurowski, Louis S. *The New Liskeard Story*. Cobalt, ON: Highway Book Shop, 1991.

LeBourdais, D.M. *Metals and Men: The Story of Canadian Mining*. Toronto, ON: McClelland and Stewart, 1957.

Longo, Roy, ed. *Historical Highlights of Canadian Mining*. Toronto, ON: Pitt Publishing, 1973.

Macbeth, Mike. *Silver Threads among the Gold*. Toronto, ON: Trans–Canada Press, 1987.

MacDowell, Laurel Sefton. *Remember Kirkland Lake: The Gold Miner's Strike of 1941-42*. Toronto, ON: University of Toronto Press, 1983.

Mallette, Beverly Dixon. *Jessica*. Cobalt, ON: Highway Book Shop, 1991.

McClelland-Wierzbicki, Kathy. *The Great Depression in Northern Ontario 1929-1934*. Sudbury, ON: Laurentian Historical Library, 1975.

McFarlane, Leslie. *A Kid in Haileybury*. Cobalt, ON: Highway Book Shop, 1975.

The Milling of Canadian Ores. 6th Commonwealth Mining and Metallurgical Congress, 1957.

Mining in Canada. 6th Commonwealth Mining and Metallurgical Congress, 1957.

Morton, Desmond. *Working People: A History of the Canadian Labour Movement*. Ottawa, ON: Deneau Publishers, 1980.

Murphy, John P. *Yankee Take-Over at Cobalt*. Cobalt, ON: Highway Book Shop, 1977.

Nelles, H.V. *The Politics of Development: Forests, Mines and Hydro-Electric Power in Ontario 1849-1941*. Toronto, ON: Macmillan of Canada, 1974.

Roberts, Wayne. *A Miner's Life: Bob Miner and the Union Organizing in Timmins, Kirkland Lake and Sudbury*. Hamilton, ON: McMaster University, 1977.

Smith, Phillip. *Harvest from the Rock: A History of Mining in Ontario*. Toronto, ON: Macmillan of Canada, 1986.

Solski, Mike and John Smaller. *Mine Mill: The History of the International Union of Mine, Mill and Smelter Workers of Canada since 1895*. Ottawa, ON: Steel Rail Publishing, 1985.

Stopps, Winnifred. *A Walk through Cobalt's Past*. Cobalt, ON: Cobalt's 75th Anniversary Miner's Festival Committee, 1978.

Swift, Jamie. *The Big Nickel: INCO at Home and Abroad*. Toronto, ON: Between the Lines, 1977.

Tataryn, Lloyd. *Dying for a Living: The Politics of Industrial Death*. Ottawa, ON: Deneau and Greenberg, 1979.

Thomson, J. E. *Willet G. Miller: Ontario's First Provincial Geologist*. Toronto, ON: Ontario Department of Mines, 1970.

Tucker, Albert. *Steam into Wilderness*. Toronto, ON: Fitzhenry and Whiteside, 1978.

Wetjen, Andre and L. H. T. Irvine. *The Kirkland Lake Story*. Cobalt, ON: Highway Book Shop, 1988.

Young, Scott and Astrid Young. *O'Brien: From Water Boy to One Million a Year*. Burnstown, ON: General Store Publishing House, 1967.